Stated Memory

Studies in German Literature, Linguistics, and Culture

Edited by James Hardin
(*South Carolina*)

THOMAS C. FOX

STATED MEMORY

EAST GERMANY AND THE HOLOCAUST

CAMDEN HOUSE

First published 1999
by Camden House

Camden House is an imprint of Boydell & Brewer Inc.
PO Box 41026, Rochester, NY 14604–4126 USA
and of Boydell & Brewer Limited
PO Box 9, Woodbridge, Suffolk IP12 3DF, UK

ISBN: 1–57113–129–9

Library of Congress Cataloging-in-Publication Data

Fox, Thomas C.
    Stated memory : East Germany and the Holocaust / Thomas C. Fox.
    p.   cm. – (Studies in German literature, linguistics, and culture)
    Includes bibliographical references and index.
    ISBN 1–57113–129–9 (alk. paper)
    1. Jews – Germany (East) 2. Holocaust survivors – Germany (East) -
-History. 3. Holocaust, Jewish (1939–1945) – Study and teaching -
-Germany (East) 4. Arts, German—Germany (East) 5. Holocaust,
Jewish (1939–1945), in motion pictures. 6. Holocaust, Jewish
(1939–1945), in literature. 7. Holocaust, Jewish (1939–1945) -
- Historiography. 8. Germany (East) – Ethnic relations. 9. Germany
(East) – Politics and government. I. Title. II. Series: Studies in German
literature, linguistics, and culture (Unnumbered)
DS135.G332F69 1998
943.1'004924—dc21   98–36112
                                                                        CIP

This publication is printed on acid-free paper.
Printed in the United States of America

Grateful acknowledgment is made to the following publishers for use, in revised form, of
the author's previously published material:

German Life and Letters for "A 'Jewish Question' in GDR Literature?" *German Life
    and Letters* 44, no. 1 (1990): 58–70.
The University of Michigan Press for *Border Crossings: An Introduction to East German
    Prose*. Ann Arbor: U of Michigan P, 1993.

Grateful acknowledgment is made for permission to print the following material:

Archiv, Gedenkstätte Buchenwald/Stiftung Gedenkstätten Buchenwald und Mittel-
    bau-Dora for "Die befreiten Häftlinge" by Fritz Cremer.
Fotothek der Mahn- und Gedenkstätte Ravensbrück/Stiftung Brandenburgische
    Gedenkstätten for the photograph of "Ältere Frau" by Will Lammert and
    "Frauenplastik" by Fritz Cremer.
Oranienburg, Gedenkstätte und Museum Sachsenhausen, Fotothek for the photo-
    graph of the obelisk.
University of South Carolina Press for "Traces in the Sand" by Johannes Bobrowski.

Contents

Illustrations

Acknowledgments

I began the research for this book under the auspices of a research grant from the Alexander von Humboldt-Stiftung. Professor Ulrich Profitlich from the FU Berlin sponsored me during my stay in Germany, which unfortunately had to be cut short. I am very grateful to the Humboldt-Stiftung and to Professor Profitlich for their generosity. I acknowledge with gratitude further support from the German Academic Exchange Service (DAAD) and the College of Arts and Sciences of The University of Alabama.

I thank the helpful staffs of the two libraries of the Jewish Community in Berlin, the libraries and archives at the Buchenwald, Ravensbrück, and Sachsenhausen memorial sites, and the *Bundesfilmarchiv* in Berlin. Robin Ostow and Thomas Jung were kind enough to read my manuscript; I value their suggestions. I am also grateful to my colleagues in German at The University of Alabama, as well as Mary Ann Smith, for their support which they have expressed in many ways.

My family provided me much sustenance as I wrote this book. My parents-in-law, Lothar and Elfriede Fischer, proved remarkably generous during my summer sojourns in Germany, as did Dr. Alois Biller. Without the unstinting help of my mother, Margaret Fox, especially with regard to child care, I could not have completed this book. I cannot begin to express my enormous gratitude to my wife, Barbara Fischer. Herself a Germanist, she has helped me in countless ways, and her presence made my numerous dreary visits to concentration camp memorials more bearable. This book is for her and our daughter Katharina, whose interruptions were numerous and, in retrospect, treasured.

T. C. F.
October 1998

For Barbara and Katharina

Introduction:
Stating German Holocaust Memory

> *Memory is never shaped in a vacuum; the motives of memory are never pure.*
>
> James Young

Performed in 1945 in the Soviet Sector of Berlin, Gotthold Ephraim Lessing's classic *Nathan der Weise* (Nathan the Wise, 1779) was the first postwar play staged in Germany, and it remained one of the most frequently produced theater pieces in East and West Germany. The reasons are obvious: in Nathan, Germans have the figure — created by a German — of the good, wise, and forgiving Jew. Nathan preaches and practices religious tolerance. His famous parable of the rings — which refuses to privilege one religion over another — represents a piece of European Enlightenment projected back into the play's setting in twelfth-century Jerusalem.

With the rise of postmodern thinking, there have been extended and often bitter discussions as to whether National Socialism and Auschwitz represent aberrations in the development of a generally beneficent Western civilization (the latter neatly symbolized by Lessing and his Nathan), or whether, with such postmodernists as Jean-François Lyotard, one should emphasize those features that connect — and be it in a perverse fashion — Auschwitz with the Enlightenment modern (Huyssen 10). Postmodernist, post-Auschwitz stagings of *Nathan der Weise* interrogate Lessing's Enlightenment-based optimism: one thinks of Claus Peymann's 1981 West German production, the conclusion of which underscores the Jew's isolation. One thinks, too, of Holocaust survivor's George Tabori's *Nathans Tod* (Nathan's Death), performed in Munich in 1991. Tabori's production adroitly shifts the emphasis from the "exhausted" ring parable of religious tolerance to the Christian Patriarch's angry declaration: "The Jew must burn!" Similarly, East German playwright Heiner Müller's *Leben Gundlings Friedrich von Preußen Lessings Schlaf Traum Schrei* (Gundling's Life Frederick of Prussia Lessing's Sleep Dream Scream) declares Lessing's ideal of Jewish-Christian tolerance to be bankrupt. Müller's Nathan recites the ring parable in an automobile junkyard littered with lifeless cultural icons, located somewhere in a desert in Montana. Before Nathan can finish he is attacked and murdered by Emilia Galotti, another of Lessing's figures; directly thereafter a blinding white light suggests an atomic inferno. But Müller's play, which had its West German premiere in 1979, could not be performed in East Germany until shortly before the end of that country.

Wrapped in a self-imposed isolation from postmodernist theory, the German Democratic Republic (East Germany, or GDR) ignored or resisted (until 1988) Müller's revisions of Lessing. It adhered to traditional stagings of *Nathan der Weise*, a piece that from 1945 until well into the 1980s was present without interruption in East German theaters (Feinberg 148). By the 1970s Lessing's Jew remained practically the only Jewish figure on East German stages (Feinberg 65). Viewing itself as the near culmination of Western History, the GDR reserved for itself the inheritance of a Locke or a Lessing, according to which religion would essentially fade away within a higher order marked by humanism, universalism, and enlightenment. Many German-Jewish intellectuals participated in the attempt to build that new and more perfect world. They perceived the socialist movement as a kind of melting pot, to paraphrase a metaphor from Arnold Zweig's novel *Traum ist teuer* (The Dream Is Dear, 1961), that would render their "difference," their Jewishness irrelevant. From socialism they derived a sense of togetherness, a feeling of belonging conjured by the writing of East German author Stephan Hermlin, and which Frank Stern, a western German scholar who teaches in Tel Aviv, characterizes as "an ongoing motif in the works of German-Jewish writers since the time of the Enlightenment" (60). Yet the Enlightenment project has always carried within itself a paradox, one played out in the GDR as well. What one Lessing scholar writes of bourgeois society applied, *mutatis mutandis*, to East German socialism as well: "In order to participate in an imminent order of civilization, to become a citizen of the future bourgeois state, 'the Jew' was expected, in effect, to gradually shed his Jewishness. Only by renouncing the cultural identity and religious practices that marked him as an 'other' — in short, only by ceasing to be traditionally Jewish — could the Jew be tolerated by the German bourgeois subject" (B. Fischer 35–36). As American scholar

Sander Gilman has noted, such thinking leads to a double bind, and to self-hatred:

> On the one hand is the liberal fantasy that anyone is welcome to share in the power of the reference group if he abides by the rules that define that group. But these rules are the very definition of the Other. The Other comprises precisely those who are not permitted to share power within the society. Thus outsiders hear an answer from their fantasy: Become like us — abandon your difference — and you may be one with us. On the other hand is the hidden qualification of the internalized reference group, the conservative curse: The more you are like me, the more I know the true value of my power, which you wish to share, and the more I am aware that you are but a shoddy counterfeit, an outsider. All of this plays itself out within the fantasy of the outsider. Yet it is not merely an artifact of marginality, for the privileged group, that group defined by the outsider as a reference for his or her own identity, wishes both to integrate the outsider (and remove the image of its own potential loss of power) and to distance him or her (and preserve the reification of its power through the presence of the powerless).
>
> (*Jewish* 2)

What this means in our context is that East Germans of Jewish descent could look, dress, talk, and act like other East Germans. They could join the Party and eschew Zionism. But many remained somehow outsiders, both in their own eyes and in those of their fellow citizens. When East German citizens insisted on their Jewishness, their sense of alterity could increase dramatically. Helmut Eschwege, a Jewish East German historian, entitled his autobiography *Fremd unter meinesgleichen* (A Stranger amongst Those like Me, 1991). A younger East German Jew told his US interviewers: "The problem for me is that I cannot say who I am, where I belong. I don't fit" (Borneman 248). And: "I am a cow in a barn for horses" (Borneman 255).

The theory and practice of East German socialism bore within themselves aspects of Lyotard's nightmare modern. With the confidence and security promised them by their *grand récit*, East German politicians repressed difference of all kinds: of class, of foreign-cosmopolitanism, of religion, of philosophy. Within the metanarrative of Marxism, East German historians constructed the master narrative of German Communism. American historian Jeffrey Herf contends of East Germany: "As in the entire history of German Communism, anti-Semitism and the Jewish catastrophe remained

marginal to the master narrative of class struggle, resistance, and re-
demption."[1] Relegated to the periphery of discourse, many East
German Marxists of Jewish descent acceded to the attempts to eradi-
cate their residues of otherness. French scholar Sonja Combe asserts
that "the Party had become their family, and the Communist culture
their refuge. This culture allowed Jews with the impulse to assimilate
to suppress their otherness, but also their Jewish suffering. Their political engagement and their Communist identity erased their
Jewishness. For the price of silence about Auschwitz in public life,
they were successful in mastering their memories . . . " (147). Frank
Stern writes that "those German Jews who returned to East Germany, even when denying their Jewishness, were still pursuing the
'modern notion of the future as progress' and intended to reorgan-
ize the 'structure of temporality' according to their memory and to
their critical conception of past failures" (71). But the efforts to live
in tolerance through attempted erasure of difference faltered in the
GDR as they had in previous German states. Despite their "impulse
to assimilate," East German citizens of Jewish descent found themselves over and again identified as Jews: during the anti-Zionist persecutions in the 1950s, or when pressured to speak out against Israel, or when the GDR played the "Jewish card" in an attempt to
improve relations with the United States. East German Jews discov-
ered — and this is a recurring theme in the writing of East German
author Jurek Becker — the truth of Sartre's dictum that a Jew is one
whom others consider a Jew.

"Am I a Jew?" demands a character in *Der Boxer* (The Boxer,
1976), a novel by Becker (251). The character, a Holocaust survivor, is protesting the insistence of his East German interlocutor, as
well as other members of East German society, on labeling him Jewish. Although I will emphasize the East German situation in this
study, it is worth noting that Western observers participate in this
exercise as well, though in a different fashion and for different reasons. Frank Stern's statement, quoted above, that East German Jews
denied their Jewishness, can stand as representative and could be
multiplied. To cite just a few examples: the author Wolf Biermann,
whose Jewish-Communist father was murdered in Auschwitz, rarely
wrote about Judaism while a citizen of East Germany. After living
for many years in the West, however, he criticized a former East
German acquaintance for being a "Jew" who "vehemently denied
that he was Jewish" (105–106). American scholar Jeffrey Peck refers

to Czech politician Rudolf Slánský and East German politician Albert Norden as Jews, though it is doubtful that either considered himself to be Jewish ("East" 454–55); likewise, Jeffrey Herf characterizes Norden and East German politician Alexander Abusch as Jews.[2] British scholar Paul O'Doherty speaks of East German "atheist Jews," "non-practising Jews," and "non-religious Jews" without, and here he is hardly alone, actually saying what constitutes Jewishness;[3] he does say that it is unclear to what extent many East German "Jews" considered themselves Jewish (*Portrayal* 25). Konrad Kwiet and Helmut Eschwege, West and East German historians who edited a book on Jewish resistance in the Third Reich, begin simply with a religious definition: a Jew is someone who chooses to belong to the Jewish Community. In the next sentence, however, they discard that definition, for it cannot account for many people of Jewish descent who continue to be regarded as Jews (19–20).

East Germans followed Communist tradition in that, officially at any rate, Judaism was a religion.[4] In this study I have tried to respect the insistence of numerous non-religious East Germans that their Jewish backgrounds made no "difference," while emphasizing the problematic nature of such desire in a Germany after Hitler and with Stalin. I characterize as Jews those who, for religious, ethnic, cultural, or political reasons consider(ed) themselves to be Jewish, and use the term "of Jewish descent" for those who did not. I am aware that this solution is not ideal.

The Cold War produced partisan historiography about the Second World War on both sides of the ideological divide. Only after 1989, for example, have western historians revisited such issues as the extent of anti-Semitism among Germans in the Second World War, or the degree of German army involvement in Nazi war crimes. A new Germany is calling for a new history, and that history is being inscribed in the tensions resulting from the attempted integration of five new German states — the former East Germany — into the former West Germany.

Both Germanys had been countries or half-nations in search of identity, and the Holocaust was never a welcome element in that identity. West Germany[5] under Chancellor Konrad Adenauer was characterized by repression and denial regarding the Holocaust, although it did, against popular opinion, agree to pay reparations to Israel. (In exchange, West Germany gained a measure of international acceptance and was allowed to join NATO). West Germany also maintained, despite the myth of a new beginning implied by the popular term "Zero Hour," a distressing continuity of National Socialist professionals in the government, teaching profession, and the judiciary; these professionals were obviously not interested in a public project of analysis, remembrance, and mourning (Herbert, "Zweierlei" 10, 15). The zeitgeist began to change in the 1960s with the highly publicized Frankfurt/Main trials of Germans who had worked at Auschwitz, with Peter Weiss's masterful but controversial play based on those trials, *Die Ermittlung* (The Investigation, 1965), or Rolf Hochhuth's *Der Stellvertreter* (The Deputy, 1963), which accuses the Pope of collusion with the Nazis and their genocidal policies. The student movement of the later 1960s and early 1970s, often and rightly seen in part as a rebellion against the silence of the older generation regarding the Second World War, changed West German society in a profound and lasting fashion.

The 1970s in West Germany were marked by a growing interest, on both the scholarly and the grass roots level, in the Holocaust, although Bundestag debates on the statute of limitations for Nazi crimes, or the surprisingly positive response in 1979 to the American television series *Holocaust*, demonstrated the continuing brisant nature of the topic and the need for further information, respectively. In the 1980s President Richard von Weizsäcker's address to the Bundestag forty years after the war was widely hailed for its inclusiveness regarding victims' groups (for instance, Communists, Sinti and Roma, Jehovah's Witnesses, homosexuals), but several Members of Parliament demonstratively left the chambers. Also in the 1980s German grass roots movements began to research the Nazi past of local communities. The resistance they sometimes encountered is recorded in the film *Das schreckliche Mädchen* (The Nasty Girl, 1990), based on a true story in Passau, Bavaria.

In the mid-1980s German historian Ernst Nolte initiated a vehement "Historians' Debate" with his suggestion that Hitler's crimes were a response to earlier atrocities committed by the Soviets; he viewed the murder of the Jews as an "Asiatic act" learned from Stalin. Other notable moments from the later 1980s and the 1990s include the controversy surrounding the Berlin monument to members of the Reichstag murdered by the Nazis. Christian Democrats balked at putting the party affiliation of the murdered parliamentarians on the monument (most had been Communists or Social Democrats), but in the end the affiliations were included. In November 1988 the Christian Democrat Philipp Jenninger, commemorating the 1938 "*Kristallnacht*" in a speech to the West German Parliament, recalled many of the positive feelings that Germans had had about Hitler in the early 1930s. The resulting national and international outrage occasioned his resignation as Speaker of the House of Parliament.

After German unification in 1990, numerous committees and the German Federal government debated how to construct Germany's first — and belated — national Holocaust memorial in the new capital of Berlin. Victims' groups vied with each other for representation while scholars and journalists argued whether the memorial should address postwar Germans, international visitors, or victims. In 1996 the German translation of Daniel Goldhagen's *Hitler's Willing Executioners* was extensively and heatedly discussed in Germany. Goldhagen argues for a far greater degree of virulent anti-Semitism among the prewar German population than has heretofore been assumed, and insists that Germans gladly murdered Jews. Although many scholars contest Goldhagen's theories, methods, and findings, ordinary Germans demonstrated considerable support for the author when he visited German cities to discuss the book.

Such controversies are, depending on one's point of view, scandalous, absurd, or pitiful, but they have proved crucial in generating a German discourse on the Holocaust. In general it is possible to argue that, despite denial and ever-present resistance, the West Germans indeed developed an important dialogue on the subject.[6] The dialogue will certainly continue in the united Germany, for the incorporation of the GDR brings the challenge of a different historical way of seeing. A German historical commission responsible for redesigning East German concentration camp memorials asserted, for example, that a West German self-examination would also be necessary (Ministerium 221), and historian Stephanie Endlich, who criticized the historical blind spots of East German memorials, noted deficiencies in West German counterparts as well (114). The new history occasioned by the new Germany will have to meet the challenge of the lingering power of East Germany's self-staging as an antifascist state.

Although scholars have devoted a great deal of attention to the ideology of East German antifascism, relatively little — and even less in English — has been written on the fashion in which the East German state, and its citizens, responded to the Holocaust. Using approaches inspired by culture studies and German studies, this book presents a first interdisciplinary attempt to trace the parameters of that response. I am writing for an educated general public,[7] but my research should also help fill gaps in existing scholarship and provide new impetus for specialists in East German and Holocaust studies.

With the verb in my title I want to denote the process by which East Germans articulated Holocaust memory, inscribing it into the East German imagination. "Stated" can be an adjective as well, in the sense of "fixed or regular" (although, as we shall see, memory oscillates and refuses to be "penned in"). Finally, *Stated Memory* connotes the role of the East German *state* itself in the construction of memory; *Webster's* defines "to state" as "to set by regulation or authority." I am concerned with the state in as well as of memory.

In this book I examine representative East German responses to the Holocaust. In the first chapter I review the Holocaust master narrative constructed by historians and the popularization and dissemination of that narrative in school texts. In the next, I examine the fashion in which the official history became, literally, "concretized" (and further popularized) in the monuments and exhibitions of the East German concentration camp memorials. The third investigates the situation of those who lived the contradictions of East German Holocaust discourse: East German Jews and people of Jewish descent. Chapter 4 analyses works by writers and filmmakers who both contributed to that discourse and at times laid bare its contradictions. I show that the East German state, with its tightly controlled public sphere, attempted to organize, censor, and orchestrate Holocaust discourse in a massive effort to utilize the "Jewish question" for its own political ends. In this I am continuing the efforts of Dan Diner, Ralph Giordano, Antonia Grunenberg, Lutz Niethammer, and others to demystify the East German antifascist program by focusing on an aspect of that program — Holocaust discourse — that those critics have generally neglected.

At the same time, one needs to emphasize that regardless of the appropriation, exploitation, and ultimate devaluation of antifascist or, in this case, Holocaust discourse by the East German state, individual citizens participated in those discourses out of a variety of motives ranging from opportunism to idealism. Characterizing antifascism as a feeling and a way of life, Frank Stern writes: "German antifascism was not only an ideology that soon became instrumentalized for the purposes of creating a society that should be molded according to the Soviet model. Antifascism was also the basic context of the lives, aspirations, and activities of those who had decided to contribute to the development of a just and democratic society in the East" (64). Artists participated actively in both aspects of that antifascist discourse. They served the state, but within the very exigencies of artistic forms they presented, sometimes consciously, at other times less so, the most differentiated East German views of the Holocaust.

The GDR utilized every opportunity to define itself as an antifascist state.[8] It accepted without question the definition of fascism developed in the 1930s by Bulgarian Communist Georgi Dimitrov for the Communist International (Comintern): fascism is the chauvinist response of the most reactionary elements of finance capital to the Communist challenge. This definition allowed the East German Socialist Unity Party (*Sozialistische Einheitspartei Deutschlands*, or SED) to argue that by breaking with capitalism it had effected a clean break with fascism and the German past. Like the Federal Republic, it too insisted on speaking of a new beginning, a "Zero Hour." The Comintern definition also permitted the GDR to proclaim that the capitalist Federal Republic was a proto- or neo-Nazi state, a breeding ground for future wars. The undeniable fact that many former Nazis fled to the Federal Republic, where West German law could or would not incarcerate them, placed a patina of respectability on such claims.[9]

East German historians argued that German capitalists brought Hitler to power in order to prevent a Communist victory. The Communists were therefore commemorated not only as the first, but also as the most important victims of Nazism. Such constructs left no room for the centrality of racism and especially anti-Semitism in Nazi ideology. In this the GDR continued a tradition of Marxist thought.[10]

The historian Konrad Kwiet asserts that "the 'classics' of scientific socialism had given relatively little attention to the 'Jewish Question' and antisemitism, which they had never regarded as 'autonomous phenomena'" ("Historians" 179). Martin Jay makes the same point: "The more radical the Marxist, the less interested in the specificity of the Jewish Question" (288). Jay notes that Max Horkheimer's essay "Die Juden und Europa" (The Jews and Europe), written in 1939, subsumes anti-Semitism under the crisis of capitalism; Horkheimer even suggests that Nazi anti-Semitic propaganda was directed more at external audiences than internal ones. (Christoph Hein criticizes such attitudes in *Passage*, his 1987 play about Walter Benjamin, in which Communists dismiss rumors that Jews are being gassed and indeed wish to suppress such rumors). In general, Marxists have considered anti-Semitism (like misogyny or xenophobia) a peripheral phenomenon, one caused by manipulation from above in order to provide a scapegoat for anti-capitalist sentiment, thus displacing the energies of class struggle. *Meyers Neues Lexikon*, published in 1972 in Leipzig, defined anti-Semitism as the "hostile feeling toward and persecution of Jews. It serves to distract the masses from the abuses of an exploitative system" (368). Konrad Kwiet writes that most German socialists believed that "the 'Jewish Question' and antisemitism were a problem of the bourgeoisie that would be automatically resolved through the overthrow of the capitalist order" ("Historians" 189).

In the late 1940s the debate was still open. In the early years of the Soviet Occupation Zone, the membership of the VVN (*Verein der Verfolgten des Nazismus* or Organization of the Persecuted of Nazism) maintained a range of viewpoints. At a 1946 commemoration of the Nazi November pogrom, participants could still wave Zionist flags and sing Hebrew songs (Timm, "9. November" 248). In 1947 the eastern German DEFA (*Deutsche Film-Aktiengesellchaft*) studios released the film *Ehe im Schatten* (Marriage in the Shadow), which describes with considerable sympathy the story of a German-Jewish actress and her German husband who are driven to suicide by the Nazis. *Affaire Blum*, a DEFA film of 1948, recounts critically a famous case of anti-Semitism during the Weimar Republic. In 1949 Stephan Hermlin published two newspaper features and a poem based on his visits to Auschwitz and the ruins of the Warsaw Ghetto. In "Hier liegen die Gesetzgeber" (Here Lie the Lawmakers), the article on the Ghetto, he traces a history of Jewish heroism, and includes Marx as a Jew. Yet already one sees the Cold War shaping Hermlin's response to Auschwitz. He speaks of a Polish survivor saved by a German who had fought with the Republicans in Spain; he not incidentally hears of a US tourist who believes Auschwitz to be nothing but propaganda; and he asks himself "as so many times before, what else would have happened without the Red Army."[11]

Jewish victims had advocates in at least one of the groups contending for power in the fledgling GDR: the exiles returning from the West. The high-ranking Communist functionary Paul Merker, who had spent the war in Mexico, was especially outspoken on the necessity of paying reparations to Jews. (Despite numerous assertions to the contrary, Merker was not of Jewish descent). Other East German citizens who spoke in favor of reparations included historian Siegbert Kahn, Leo Zuckermann (who would be President Wilhelm Pieck's chief of staff between 1949 and 1951), Julius Meyer (who would become a Member of Parliament, Chair of East Berlin's Jewish Community, and Director of the Organization of East German Jews), and also Otto Grotewohl, leader of the Social Democrats in the Soviet Zone. This group was opposed by many of the Communists who had endured the Second World War in concentration camps, prisons, or in the underground and who had occasionally unconsciously internalized the Nazi concentration camp hierarchy. For them, Jews had been passive, unorganized, and — for some this was the logical conclusion — at least in part themselves to blame for their fate. Apparently viewing memory as a "zero-sum game" (Herf, "German Communism" 293), this constellation of Communists strongly opposed the commemoration of any group they felt would serve to relativize or hide their own martyrdom or suffering. Their efforts in fact briefly shut out Jews from any recognition as victims of fascism (Groehler, "Umgang" 42–43; "Holocaust" 48; "Juden" 53–54).

A third power group consisted of the Moscow exiles led by Party Chief Walter Ulbricht. Ulbricht faithfully followed (and sometimes exceeded) the Soviet Party line with all its tactical swerves and feints; these included anti-Jewish measures. By the early 1950s at the latest, the Ulbricht group was firmly in charge. Ulbricht purged many members of the first and second groups, which did not prevent the GDR from instrumentalizing the antifascist involvement of the second group to a state supporting foundation myth.[12] But it is important to remember that in the grid of East German discourses on the

Holocaust, the positions of all three groups were somehow always present.

In the 1950s the Stalinist anti-Zionist campaign affected all East bloc countries. The Czech show trial of 1952 against Slánský, a leading Communist government official of Jewish descent, was observed carefully in the GDR, and a long paper on its "lessons" circulated among SED members. Paul Merker, who had been relieved of his functions in 1950, was imprisoned and tried as a Zionist agent. "Contact with otherness of various kinds," Jeffrey Herf writes of Merker, "proved dangerous in the formative years of the GDR" ("German Communism" 287). The state directed numerous measures against Jews, people of Jewish descent, and their supporters: house searches, searches of the Jewish Communities, interrogations, and background checks. Many of the people affected fled to the West. In 1953 the government disbanded the VVN and replaced it with the more malleable Antifascist Committee. The GDR refused to pay restitution of any kind to Jewish victims of Nazism or to return Jewish property that had been confiscated by the Nazis.[13] This atmosphere did not encourage much thinking about the Holocaust in the GDR, and it was in the wake of such actions — and reflecting them — that the three major East German concentration camp memorials were designed and opened: Buchenwald (1958), Ravensbrück (1959), and Sachsenhausen (1961).

In the second half of the 1950s the GDR used the Holocaust, especially in literature and film, as a vehicle to show that many former Nazis were living safely in the Federal Republic and that some had attained high positions there.[14] In May 1960 the arrest of Adolf Eichmann by the Israeli Secret Service focused worldwide attention on Nazi crimes, and the GDR seized this opportunity to intensify its propaganda attacks on West Germany. The most prominent target was Hans Globke, director of the Chancellor's office. As a Nazi judge Globke had written an approving commentary on the racist Nuremberg Laws of 1935. In Sachsenhausen, opened in 1961, a small special exhibition on the Nazi persecution of the Jews was included, with Globke and other West Germans assuming inordinate space. In 1991 a German historical commission characterized the exhibition as provisional and dilettantish (Ministerium 236); indeed, it was hurriedly gathered after the Eichmann arrest. There was no similar exhibit at Buchenwald or Ravensbrück, both of which opened earlier.

The Arab-Israeli conflicts and Israeli conquests constituted important aspects of the official East German discourse on the Holocaust, and the actions of the "Zionist Aggressor-State Israel" found regular comparison with the Nazis.[15] This was not the case from the beginning. The Soviet Union had supported the creation of Israel in 1948, and Germans in the Soviet Occupation Zone sided with the new state during its war of independence. Writing for the East German magazine *Weltbühne* in 1949, Karl-Eduard von Schnitzler, who would later become a leading television commentator in the GDR, condemned the Egyptian army for maintaining advisors from the Nazi *Afrikakorps*:

> Among the troop leaders we find SS-officer Katzmann, who formerly commanded a special police division in Poland and who was a specialist for the extermination of the Jews. Now he wages war against Israel . . . . Imagine what it means today when people guilty of crimes against humanity, who have hundreds of thousands of Jewish deaths on their conscience, do not stand in front of a court of law but rather as the commanders of an army that they can again lead against Jews. (Cited in Timm, "Israel" 157)

When soon thereafter the Soviet Union withdrew support from Israel, the GDR followed, and the restitution agreements of 1951–53 between Israel and the Federal Republic could be dismissed in the GDR (against the backdrop of the Slánský trial) as a business deal between West German and Israeli capitalists (for instance, *Neues Deutschland* 25 Nov. 1952). The GDR also began to build relations with Arab countries as an attempt to break through its diplomatic isolation occasioned by West Germany's Hallstein Doctrine, which said, in effect, that Bonn would not maintain diplomatic relations with any nation that recognized East Germany. During the 1956 Middle East war the GDR called on the Federal Republic to pay reparations to Egypt, because Israel was ostensibly using West German restitution money to wage war. In the mid-1960s the GDR began supplying Arab countries with weapons.[16]

The East German anti-Israeli propaganda reached a crescendo after the June 1967 war. In a cartoon published by the (East) *Berliner Zeitung* in July 1967, a resurrected Hitler observes Moshe Dayan who, armed with a machine gun, has grabbed Jerusalem and the Gaza strip. Hitler comments: "Keep it up, colleague Dayan!" Kurt Pätzold, probably the most original East German historian of the Holocaust, began writing in the 1970s, and his work is also characterized by anti-Israeli polemics, at least through the early 1980s (after which it became no longer politic). In 1981 Karl-Eduard von Schnitzler, who had earlier invoked the Holocaust to condemn the Egyptians, returned to the subject, though with different emphasis: "The government in Tel Aviv does not have the least right to use Jewish victims of German fascism as an alibi for its policies, because the regime in Tel Aviv itself acts according to the fascist lie of *Volk* without *Raum*. It steals land according to the fascist motto of *Blut und Boden*. It leads an annihilation campaign against the Arab people of Palestine, a policy of extermination" (Cited in Mertens, "Staatlich" 144). The East German historian Joachim Petzold, writing in 1984 on the Third Reich, dismisses those who would assert that "fascism is in its essence anti-Semitism. Such arguments are advantageous for those who today would like to free neo-fascism — as long as it is not anti-Semitic — from the odium of fascism, or for those who unwaveringly support Israel, whose Begin-Sharon government clearly used fascist methods against the Palestinians" (35). The anti-Israeli campaign impacted all aspects of Holocaust discourse. An East German book on the Nazi concentration camp Sachsenhausen published in 1967 noted that in the camp "Thousands of Jews lost their lives, died of hunger and thirst, suffocated, were murdered" (Komitee, *Damals* 83). In editions between 1970 and 1982 (that is, after the 1967 Arab-Israeli war) the sentence was changed: "Hundreds of Jews were murdered; they starved, died of thirst, and suffocated" (Komitee, *Damals* 1970: 96; Komitee, *Sachsenhausen* 1974: 99; 1977: 79; 1982: 86). Between 1965 and 1984 East German schoolbooks also did not specifically cite the six million Jews murdered by the Nazis.

In late 1978 the East Germans marked the anniversary of the 1938 Nazi November pogrom with commemorations and publications. (Unlike West Germany, however, East Germany did not broadcast the American television series *Holocaust*). Although such ceremonies were undoubtedly meaningful for many involved, they served state purposes. The introduction to a small exhibition at the German Historical Museum in East Berlin declared: "When the most reactionary parts of German finance capital brought the Hitler fascists to power, it was clear to them that they were dealing with a Party that was extremely anti-Communist, anti-democratic, and aggressive. They were also very aware of the brutally anti-Semitic character of this Party. In our exhibition we want to make this connection clear with strong emphasis" (Jüdische 65–66). In general, as many of the speeches and newspaper articles from 1978–79 demonstrate, the East German commemorations were designed to emphasize the state as the good Germany at a time when the West Germans were again debating whether to extend the statute of limitation for Nazi crimes. The East German campaign served in many respects to reprise a similar effort from 1965, which, Lothar Mertens argues, also used the "Jewish question" to further the political interests of the GDR ("Staatlich" 143).

In 1984 the East Germans updated the Buchenwald museum, but the new exhibition merely demonstrated that no real changes in the Party line were possible. Although more attention is given to anti-Semitism, and although Sinti and Roma victims are mentioned, racism remains a secondary phenomenon, and one that had, furthermore, essentially disappeared in the GDR. In the 1980s the East Germans also refused to air Claude Lanzmann's *Shoah*, a film that among other things demonstrated the continuation of anti-Semitism in East Germany's socialist neighbor Poland. But the later 1980s brought a final state-inspired commemoration of the Holocaust. Attempting once again to embarrass the Federal Republic (in 1986, Chancellor Kohl and President Reagan had met in the West German city of Bitburg and visited a cemetery that contains some SS graves), and powered by a desire to attain Most Favored Nation trade status with the United States, the GDR played its "Jewish card," commemorating the 50th anniversary of the so-called *Kristallnacht*, the 1938 pogrom, with a flood of ceremonies, publications, and proclamations. Numerous East German documentary and feature films on Jews and Nazism played in cinemas and television. This seemingly sudden change of direction was confusing to some citizens; probably in response to letters to the editor, the *Berliner Zeitung* carried a programmatic article entitled: "Did the GDR Just Now Discover the Jews?" (18/19 February 1989). There was, however, no attempt to look critically at the GDR's own history of responding to the Holocaust. Despite undeniable East German neo-Nazi and Skinhead activity, state representatives, supported by East German Jews and people of Jewish descent, proclaimed loudly that they, as opposed to the Federal Republic, had eradicated anti-Semitism and hatred of the Other in their socialist society.

After the Wall fell in November 1989, but before unification in October 1990, the new East German government under Hans Modrow attempted to resuscitate a dying state by playing on Jewish fear of a united Germany. After forty years of hostility, the GDR now sought to establish diplomatic relations with Israel.[17] For the first time, the East Germans acknowledged that as a successor state to the Third Reich they carried responsibility for Nazi victims.[18] With a gesture that was at best symbolic and at worst cynical, the bankrupt state offered to negotiate reparations. This was a final effort to instrumentalize the Holocaust for political purposes.

Notes

[1] Herf, "German Communism" 294. See also his extended discussion in *Divided Memory.*

[2] Herf, "East German" 19. For more on these two men, who in a sense epitomize the fashion in which East Germany shut down discussion of the Jewish catastrophe, see Herf, *Divided.*

[3] O'Doherty, *Portrayal* 23, 25, 55. See also his page 12: "Those who define Jewishness in terms of membership of Jewish communities and congregations, almost all of which have been Zionist in outlook since 1945 (although the GDR communities were never allowed to state this openly), are implicitly denying the Jewishness of such figures as Heinrich Heine, Ludwig Börne, Kurt Tucholsky, Karl Kraus and Lion Feuchtwanger, to name just a few. They are setting preconditions for a German-Jewish culture, one which accepts the belief that the Jews are a nation rather than a religious grouping or even a 'Schicksalsgemeinschaft,' a belief to which most pre-1933 German writers of Jewish descent would not have subscribed." This confusing formulation is revealing.

[4] For an example of the kinds of confusion this could cause between East and West, see the Borneman and Peck interview with Jürgen Kuczynski (121–134, esp. 130).

[5] For a more extended summary, see Markovits.

[6] See, for example, Deutschkron 195, Herbert, "Zweierlei" 18, or Probst 196.

[7] For this reason I have decided to use the generally accepted, if problematical, term "Holocaust" throughout this study. I have also translated German quotations into English. Unless otherwise noted, all translations are my own.

[8] For an additional overview of East German responses to the Holocaust, see Peck, "East" and Herf, *Divided.*

[9] For more on trials of former Nazis, see Grabitz and Werle. See also Buruma's comparison of the differing fashion in which Germans (East and West) and Japanese have dealt with the Second World War.

[10] See also Herf's discussion of "multiple restorations" in *Divided Memory* and Sigrid Meuschel's analysis of the fashion in which the SED utilized various discourses, including that of anti-Zionism, to provide itself legitimation.

[11] Hermlin, "Auschwitz" 88. In the two newspaper pieces and in Herm-lin's poem "Die Asche von Birkenau" (1949) (The Ashes of Birkenau), the mourning of the Jewish catastrophe is offset by the optimistic pathos of reconstruction, by what Herf would call a Hegelian moment: Socialism will now replace barbarism/capitalism/fascism. Hermlin suggests repeat-edly that the dead lie peacefully under all this socialist activity (e.g., "Auschwitz" 89), an image that recurs in "Die Zeit der Gemeinsamkeit" (The Time Together).

[12] For more on the foundation myth, see Niethammer.

[13] For detailed discussions of these issues, see Goschler or Schüler. See also the studies of Jews in the GDR that appeared as this book was in the editing process: Jutta Illichmann, *Die DDR und die Juden. Die deutsch-landpolitische Instrumentalisierung von Juden und Judentum durch die Partei- und Staatsführung der SBZ/DDR von 1945 bis 1990*. Frankfurt: Lang, 1997; Lothar Mertens, *Davidstern unter Hammer und Zirkel. Die jüdischen Gemeinden in der SBZ/DDR und ihre Behandlung durch Partei und Staat 1945–1990*. Hildesheim: Georg Olms Verlag, 1997; Angelika Timm, *Hammer, Zirkel, Davidstern. Das gestörte Verhältnis der DDR zu Zionismus und Staat Israel*. Bonn: Bouvier, 1997.

[14] See for example the films *Zwischenfall in Benderath, Der Prozeß wird vertagt, Ein Tagebuch für Anne Frank*, or Keller's play *Begegnung 57.*

[15] For detailed discussions, see Dittmar; Timm, "Israel"; Mertens, "Staat-lich"; or Herf, *Divided* 190–200.

[16] Groehler, "Juden" 54. Mertens asserts that arms shipments began al-ready in the 1950s ("Staatlich" 143.)

[17] Jeffrey Herf writes: "East Germany was the only Communist govern-ment in the Soviet bloc which up to 1989 did not have diplomatic rela-tions with the state of Israel. Its support for Israel's adversaries never wa-vered" (*Divided* 200).

[18] In the 1970s the East Germans had made a limited offer of reparations to Jewish victims living in the United States. The offer was refused as in-sufficient.

"Keep it up, colleague Dayan!"
Berliner Zeitung, *East Berlin, 14 July 1967*

1: The State of Memory: The Holocaust in East German Historiography

> *The primacy of antifascism ulti-*
> *mately stripped Auschwitz of its*
> *core.*
> Dan Diner

In the 1970s the historian Konrad Kwiet rightly asserted that "anti-semitism, the history of German Jews and their persecution are not themes considered worthy of study for their own sake within the terms of reference of GDR historiography" ("Historians" 173). Al-though ideological restrictions loosened in the 1980s, Kwiet's dic-tum can stand as a general comment on East German history writing through 1989. As eastern German historian Olaf Groehler points out, for historians in the GDR the Comintern theory of 1935 re-mained until 1989 "an absolute article of faith."[1] Such economic re-ductionism could not elucidate the centrality of anti-Semitism and racism for the Nazi party; at best, East German historians viewed anti-Semitism as a distraction for the masses, or as a phenomenon subsumed within the Nazi's anti-Slavism and anti-Communism. The economic paradigm could also ill explain Nazi genocide practices. Early attempts to demonstrate the economic use of slave labor fal-tered before the fact that the Nazis fanatically continued to extermi-nate Jews even when their war economy had developed a desperate need for labor. Kwiet noted in 1984 that East German historians could never adequately explain this fact (*Selbstbehauptung* 14).

During the first years of the Soviet Occupation Zone it appeared that the discussion might develop differently. Books by Siegbert Kahn or Stefan Heymann, both published in 1948, presented a somewhat more differentiated view of anti-Semitism, which they re-garded as a basic component of Nazi ideology. This is also the case in an article by Paul Merker, published on 10 November 1948 in *Neues Deutschland,* the official Party organ. According to the news-paper, the article represents a selection from Merker's book *Das Dritte Reich und sein Ende* (The Third Reich and its End), which would appear soon. It never did. As the Soviets increased repressive measures in the wake of Tito's defiance, voices like Merker's were stilled. In the early 1950s he was stripped of his functions, and in 1952 he was imprisoned as a Zionist agent. At his trial he was jeered as "King of the Jews."[2]

During the 1950s the Holocaust did not exist in East German historiography.[3] An exemplary case is the teacher's manual *Deutschland in der Zeit der faschistischen Diktatur 1933–1945* (Germany during the Period of the Fascist Dictatorship 1933–1945) by the historian Walter Bartel, a former Buchenwald inmate and one of the leaders of the Berlin chapter of the Organization of the Persecuted of Nazism. Bartel's book nowhere gives the number of murdered Jews, and other information is, according to one of his former colleagues, "cited incorrectly" (Groehler, "Umgang" 238). Bartel speaks of "1,500,000 murdered (*Ermordete*) in the concentration camp Maidanek" or of "4,000,000 murdered from many countries of Europe and the USA in the concentration camp of Auschwitz."[4] The absence of the Holocaust has several reasons. East German historians, like those in West Germany, were still very close to the event and in many ways anxious to forget it; their government (with their assistance) had after all elevated them to the "victors of history," and absolved them of guilt by pushing it westward. More important, however, the Soviet-inspired anti-Zionist campaign of the early 1950s rendered Jewish topics (and victims) extremely sensitive, as the case of Merker and others amply illustrated. Finally, the GDR was more interested in celebrating the Communist resistance — symbolized by men such as Bartel — for reasons of its own legitimization.[5]

When the Israeli secret service captured Adolf Eichmann in May 1960, Politburo member Albert Norden, a man of Jewish descent, urged Ulbricht to maximize the propaganda value in a campaign directed against the Federal Republic (Timm, "9. November" 254). East German historians quickly rediscovered the Holocaust, and three works of crude propaganda from that time exemplify, especially in their attacks on Globke, the instrumentalization of the event.[6] Star East German lawyer Friedrich Kaul (a man of Jewish descent who would later represent the GDR at the Frankfurt/Main Auschwitz trials and who plays a role in Peter Weiss's play *Die Ermittlung*) reveals his agenda at the outset of his book on Eichmann. In a conversation with the Israeli Attorney General, a conversation Kaul inserts as his book's epigraph, he exclaims: "You are only naming the dead! Why not also name those who are still living today and who have already attained official positions and honors in West Germany?" (*Der Fall*). East German historian Heinz Kühnrich published a book entitled *Judenmörder Eichmann. Kein Fall der Vergangenheit* (Jew-Murderer Eichmann. No Case of the Past) in which he accused Bonn of having protected Eichmann (11) and of preparing new genocide campaigns (14). In a second book called *Der KZ-Staat* (The Concentration Camp State), Kühnrich includes such chapters as "The SS Marches to Bonn's Pace"; "Brown Robes Protect the Bonn State"; "Nazis in Bonn's Police Force"; "Hitler's Generals Command the Bonn Army"; "SS Doctors Are Practicing Again"; "Bonn Pays the Murderers," and so on. His "analysis" of Nazi genocidal practices is primitive and propagandistic: "Auschwitz, Treblinka, Maidanek, and Theresienstadt became symbols of a brutish system that had as a goal the extermination of entire peoples in order to make a profit" (42; see also 78). Kühnrich was employed by the East German Institute for Marxism-Leninism, and his work appeared in the Party-owned Dietz Publishing house. Kühnrich's major points — that Communists were the first and most important victims of Nazism; that anti-Communism, not racism, was the major component of Nazi ideology; and that anti-Semitism was and is the expression of the profit motive of the ruling class — served, as Groehler notes, to press East German historiography into a corset and a severely circumscribed officialspeak ("Holocaust" 53). The three East German concentration camp memorials were opened around this time, and the Kühnrich/Kaul books, together with the general scholarly silence concerning the Holocaust in the 1950s, determined the standard of discourse at those sites as well. In Sachsenhausen, for example, a Kühnrich chart (which Kühnrich does not document) demonstrating the profitability of an individual slave laborer was reproduced and prominently exhibited.

Nonetheless, these books signaled the end of the Holocaust taboo in East German historiography.[7] In 1960 Siegbert Kahn published a collection of documents that demonstrated the reaction of the KPD (*Kommunistische Partei Deutschlands*, or Communist Party of Germany) to the 1938 pogroms and the KPD abhorrence of Nazi racism. In the following years these documents became a kind of dogma in themselves, and no East German publication on the Holocaust could pass the censor without reference to them. Groehler believes they assumed a kind of alibi function that served to suppress doubts or criticisms regarding Communist policy vis-à-vis Jewish persecution ("Holocaust" 52). In the former Jewish exhibition at Sachsenhausen, documents based on Kahn's work were accorded central place.

Helmut Eschwege, a Jewish-German historian living in Dresden, also seized the opportunity provided by the Eichmann trial to send a letter to Politburo member Kurt Hager and argue for the publication of a book on which he had been working for several years (Groehler, "Umgang" 242). Nonetheless, Eschwege's *Kennzeichen J* (Marker J), a series of pictures and documents dealing with the Holocaust, did not appear until several years later, in 1966. It represented a milestone of kinds, for it provides the first more comprehensive East German effort to document and analyze the persecution of the Jews. Until this point, most Eastern bloc research on the Holocaust had originated with Bernard Mark's Jewish Research Institute in Warsaw (some of it had been translated and had appeared in the GDR), and the conspicuous absence of East German research had become embarrassing at international conferences (Kwiet, "Historians" 185). Eschwege's collection of documents, although more scholarly than Kühnrich's work, generally attempts to establish the same points. But in two important respects, the book departs from the Party line, and those departures had consequences for the publication history of the work as well as for subsequent East German writing on the Holocaust.

Eschwege's publishing house attempted to protect itself by including in the book a preface by the internationally-famous East German-Jewish writer Arnold Zweig. A foreword signed by the editors of the publishing house and Eschwege furthermore keeps a cautious distance from Rudi Goguel's introduction, noting that a (later) Marxist interpretation of anti-Semitism would be necessary (8). The foreword emphasizes: "It was consciously decided not to include the centuries-old bloody history of anti-Semitism and its manifestations in other countries in order not to distract from the main point of the book: to demonstrate the responsibility of the German ruling classes — beginning with those who put Hitler in the saddle . . . " (7–8). Arnold Zweig dutifully concurs with similar words: "Corporal Adolf Hitler was put into the ruling seat of the Weimar Republic because through him German big business hoped to manage the working class . . . " (5).

Goguel's introduction reiterates this theme: even bourgeois historians, he notes, are beginning to accept the Marxist contention that the Nazis came to power as a result of class warfare (9). Some of the upper class may not have approved of Nazi anti-Semitism, but in fact profited from it through the appropriation of Jewish property and in the exploitation of Jewish workers (10). By "giving" Hitler power, the industrialists created the first conditions for genocide, and hence carry ultimate responsibility.[8] Goguel also includes the requisite attacks on revanchist West Germany, with its personnel problems (especially Globke) (12), and he concludes with the standard admonition: "As long as the [capitalist] system exists, the conditions exist for further and new mass criminality" (22). The essay ends with a hymn to socialism, under which the period of brutal persecution has finally ended, replaced by an era of "irreversible emancipation and brotherly solidarity" (23). In all of this Goguel's introduction clearly fits into the main argument of the book, and it sets the rhetorical standard for all subsequent East German writing on the Holocaust. In two important respects, however, it swerves from the Party line. To begin with, it has understanding, even friendly words for the Zionists who, Goguel acknowledges, helped a half million Jews to leave the area of German hegemony (16).

Goguel's introduction transgressed in a second way as well. Following Günter Paulus, whose book *Die zwölf Jahre des tausendjährigen Reiches* (The Twelve Years of the Thousand-Year Reich) appeared in 1965, Goguel writes: "Imperialist wars are waged primarily for the economic interests of the ruling classes . . . . However, the fanaticism with which the Nazis instituted the 'Final Solution' of the Jewish question transcended economic questions as well as wartime demands . . . " (18). Goguel thus calls into question basic tenets of Marxist theory, and also underscores the difficulty East German Marxists encountered in explaining Nazi genocide policies. He weakens his earlier argument (that capitalists supported Hitler because they profited from the exploitation of Jewish labor) when he notes: "In this case murder had primacy over exploitation. The Nazi state consciously did without desperately needed Jewish laborers — the forced labor in the extermination camps was merely a special form of extermination, and the profit [*Nutzeffekt*] was small" (18). Such remarks disrupted the main arguments of Kühnrich or of the East German concentration camp museums at Ravensbrück, Sachsenhausen, and Buchenwald, which in part reflected Kühnrich's writing. Goguel attempts to return to a Marxist argument at the conclusion of his discussion, but his helplessness is apparent, and he suggests that one must accord the Nazi state sphere "a certain independence and sovereign activity" (19). As Olaf Groehler points out, such a formulation never again occurred in East German historiography on the Holocaust ("Holocaust" 56–57). That was, he suspects, impossible, for in the same year Günter Paulus's book was strongly attacked by Party officials and withdrawn. The criticism of Paulus's book centered on his alleged failure to analyze the Nazi dictatorship sufficiently in terms of class interests. Goguel's introduction was not treated in a similar fashion, Groehler believes, since 1) the GDR needed Eschwege's book for international respectability; 2) as of 1960 the SED was making efforts to support the Jewish Communities in the GDR; and 3) it was hardly politic to attack such a book.

In late 1965, at the 11th Plenary Session of the SED, Ulbricht's heir-apparent Erich Honecker commenced a wide-ranging attack on critical East German artists and intellectuals. Intellectuals who had convinced themselves that the building of the Berlin Wall in 1961 would actually give them more freedom, because the state would feel less threatened, were rudely awakened. British scholar David Childs notes that "Honecker's attack was a general one against all those concerned with culture and the mass media in the GDR" (215–216). The government dissolved historical research groups involved in research that was ideologically suspect and instituted further repressive measures that affected all subsequent East German writing on the Holocaust (Groehler, "Holocaust" 58).

One sees the effects in *Juden unterm Hakenkreuz* (Jews under the Swastika, 1973), a collection of documents and photographs edited by East German historians Klaus Drobisch, Rudi Goguel, and Werner Müller. Although the tome presents a chronological overview of the Nazi persecution and murder of the Jews, it does not try to present these activities in any kind of new analytical framework. Indeed, the volume had originally been conceived and researched by Helmut Eschwege as a collection of texts to accompany the documents in *Kennzeichen J.* Hence the origins of *Juden unterm Hakenkreuz*, like those of *Kennzeichen J.*, date back to the 1950s. After the success of *Kennzeichen J.* an East German publisher contracted to bring out Eschwege's companion volume in 1969. The 1967 Arab-Israeli war, however, meant that a book with this theme could only appear with the approval of the Foreign Ministry, and that approval was first forthcoming in 1974. Before that, the censors had Eschwege's work thoroughly rewritten by Goguel, Drobisch, and Müller, and they, not Eschwege, appear as authors in the published version (Eschwege, *Fremd* 208–211).

Kurt Pätzold's *Faschismus-Rassenwahn-Judenverfolgung* (Fascism, Racial Insanity, Jewish Persecution), published in 1975, presented some of the first original East German research on the Holocaust. Praised for its thorough use of archival material and its rich documentation (Groehler, "Holocaust" 58; Kwiet, "Historians" 196), the book provided a detailed accounting of the beginnings of the Nazi policy towards the Jews. As Konrad Kwiet pointed out, no comparable work existed at that time in the Federal Republic ("Historians" 196).

Pätzold's work on the "political strategy and tactics of German fascist imperialism" between 1933–35 is nonetheless rendered problematic by his jeremiads against non-Marxist historians who, according to the author, employ "banal excuses" (*Ausflüchte*) and purposeful ignorance to argue for the autonomy of politics and ideology over economic factors and hence assign blame everywhere but where it belongs (10). Konrad Kwiet has responded to similar arguments with the example of Hjalmar Schacht, the Nazi "economic dictator" who, in order to prevent disruption of the economy, unsuccessfully attempted to alter Nazi persecution of Jews and aim it exclusively at Communists ("Historians" 197).

Pätzold also follows the Party line with his strong anti-Zionism. Zionists, although "certainly not they alone," helped hinder an antifascist world front, the only possibility of preventing war and genocide (277). Here Jews become in a sense responsible for their own death; such factors as the Soviet-German non-aggression pact or the prewar Communist social theory of fascism (according to which the KPD condemned the more moderate Social Democrats as fascist, hence splitting the working class and expediting Hitler's rise to power) do not and cannot figure in Pätzold's argument.

Pätzold's subsequent collection of documents from 1983, *Verfolgung, Vertreibung, Vernichtung* (Persecution, Expulsion, Extermination), was the first East German historical study addressing the Holocaust to appear in paperback. Since the publication of his dissertation in 1975, Pätzold had become the leading Party historian on the Holocaust, but his formulations in the 1980s are tired and formulaic — there is little difference between his writing in 1983 and Eschwege's from 1966. According to Pätzold, racism and anti-Semitism grew out of the Nazi desire for world domination and remained subordinate to that goal (7). Although anti-Semitism predated the Nazis, their contribution was to turn it to the service of class warfare, in that they made race appear more important than class (8–9). Anti-Semitism served as a diversion from class warfare (14), and it would only disappear with the eradication of bourgeois society (36). One problem that bourgeois Jewish functionaries had in the 1930s, according to the author, was that "misunderstanding or ignoring the class nature of fascism," they chose the wrong strategies (37). Such arguments based on the "logic of class struggle" had already figured prominently in Pätzold's earlier book (*Faschismus* 78; 277), and they blame the victim.

Pätzold encounters the same difficulties in explaining genocide as his predecessors. Can, he asks, Nazi anti-Semitism still be called capitalist-imperialist after it turns genocidal? Did that practice not actively damage business profitability? Does it not represent the victory of ideology over material interests? (*Verfolgung* 20). Pätzold dates the Nazi decision to begin wide-scale genocide with the invasion of the Soviet Union, when German leaders still believed in a quick and easy victory and employed special units to rid the occupied lands of "*Untermenschen*" and ready the territories for German settlers. Even assuming the correctness of this, it does not explain the fanatical adherence to genocide until the very end. Pätzold acknowledges this indirectly with a turgid concession that almost — but not quite — approaches Goguel's remarks of eighteen years earlier: "The identification of material interests, which were ultimately determined by the imperialist goal to which the mass murder belonged, opposes any vulgar-materialist, purely economic labeling. And it distances itself likewise from every underestimation of the relatively independent functioning of ideology" (*Verfolgung* 25).

The Humboldt University professor concludes his introduction by discussing the contemporary reception of the Holocaust. He is particularly caustic regarding "politicians of Zionism and pro-Zionist forces, supported by historians and journalists" who spread "legends" about Jews living in Germany in 1933 (*Verfolgung* 27):

> The end result is that the fascist persecution and massacre of the Jews is supposed to appear as the logical way to Israel, for whose modern imperialist policies [those forces named above] are at-

tempting to win friends and sympathizers. A historical interpretation that attempts to separate the expulsion and extermination of
the Jews from its context within an imperialist war plan . . . serves
deceitful purposes which can without doubt be compared with
those of the Nazi fascists. This applies especially to the formula:
"Anti-Zionism is modern anti-Semitism." This slogan wants to
provoke sympathy for an ideology and a politics that are at least
class-related to that of German fascism. This is not the place to in-
vestigate the methods, dodges, and tricks used by those [named
above] in their disgusting attempt to misuse the dead victims of a
past imperialist politics as a justification for contemporary anti-Arab
imperialism. (*Verfolgung* 28–29)

By utilizing a rhetoric that twice brings Israel, at least associatively,
into comparison with the Nazis, Pätzold fulfills the East German
prescription for partisan historiography.

In the 1980s Gorbachov's *glasnost* had a small influence on East
German historians, although many questions remained taboo until
1989. Eastern German historian Rainer Eckert lists just some of
them: how should one judge the KPD resistance to Nazism, inas-
much as the KPD itself rejected parliamentary democracy? Was the
KPD really the party of unyielding antifascism or did not its condemnation of the Social Democrats really hinder the struggle against
the Nazis? What were the results of the Moscow show trials? What
were the effects of Soviet spies in the Spanish Civil War? How does
one explain the Hitler-Stalin pact? What of the German antifascists
that Moscow surrendered to Germany? What of the fate of many
other German antifascist exiles in Stalin's Soviet Union? ("Ende"
89). These questions, which are intricately intertwined with any
honest exploration of the period, remained off limits to East German
historians. But in the later 1980s the need to expand trade with the
United States, plus the desire to exploit the international criticism
directed against the Federal Republic after President Reagan and
West German Chancellor Helmut Kohl visited the Bitburg cemetery
containing the graves of *Waffen*-SS, proved decisive in placing East
German historical discussions of the Holocaust in a central position.
This represented the final stage in East German historians' instrumentalization of the event.

Despite the state-inspired origins of the East German discussion
in the later 1980s (culminating in the 1988 commemoration of the
1938 November pogrom), the discourse demonstrates more openness and sensitivity than previous efforts. Attacks on Israel are rare.

One finds more attention to the role of the German people and other perpetrators, and a willingness to recognize more victims. In his introduction to a collection of documents on the November pogrom, Kurt Pätzold admitted that Jewish Communists and Social Democrats suffered more than their non-Jewish comrades (*Kristallnacht* 75). Writing of Auschwitz, Rudolf Hirsch and Rosemarie Schuder noted: "It was mostly Jews who were murdered here. Also Sinti and Roma, called Gypsies. And also soldiers of the Red Army. And resistance fighters of all nations" (730). Irene Runge commented on the Nazi "hatred of Jews, Communists, Social Democrats, Gypsies, Masons, and homosexuals," and on the "hatred against and persecution of all those who thought or lived differently" (*Kristallnacht* 15).

That Runge was working with the East German secret police and hence herself involved in persecuting those who thought differently was only revealed after 1989. But much in the East German discourse of the 1980s serves to remind one of the hypocrisy of that discourse, and of the frozen nature adhering to East German historiography on the Holocaust. Pätzold continues to view anti-Semitism as a diversion for class conflict (*Kristallnacht* 48) and celebrates the Soviet Union while jousting with France, England, and the United States (*Kristallnacht* 98–99, 104). Hirsch and Schuder end their investigation of the roots and effects of anti-Semitism in Germany with a long chapter on IG Farben, the firm that built factories at Auschwitz and also supplied the Zyklon-B for the gas chambers. "Many of them [former industrialists during the Nazi period] are sitting comfortably even today, honored and highly decorated with awards from the Federal Republic, in Frankfurt/Main, Hoechst, Ludwigshafen, Leverkusen, and Essen. Those who profited from [the Auschwitz] train connection and the slaves, they are living in Germany, in the other part" (730–731). The sentences are not incorrect but they are one-sided. By blending out the problematic reception of the Holocaust in the GDR, the authors' indignation carries little credibility.

The Holocaust in East German Schoolbooks

The depiction of the Holocaust in East German schoolbooks of course mirrors that of the more "scholarly" work, although in the textbooks — as in the concentration camp memorials — the instrumentalization becomes more pronounced. The schoolbooks are designed to teach, but also to persuade, and they present the SED Party line, including the exigencies of East German foreign policy, in distilled fashion.[9] As with other official history writing, East German school texts deny anti-Semitism or racism its central role in Nazi ideology, and discussions of Nazi anti-Jewish activity are often coupled with, or subsumed and relativized by reference to Nazi slaughter of Poles and Russians. The long history of anti-Semitism in Germany is only mentioned in later textbooks, and the authors of the textbooks, like those of the concentration camp museum exhibitions, are clearly uncomfortable with the active participation of the German masses, including workers, in anti-Semitic activities. The difficulty East German historians experienced in viewing Jews as a category outside class or nationality is evident; Robin Ostow points out that the indexes for schoolbooks from 1984 and 1988 contain the entry "Persecution of the Jews" but none for Jews themselves. "There is no information as to who the Jews were, or where they came from" ("Persecution" 5). In the entire 10-year curriculum of East German schools, two hours were reserved for the study of the persecution of the Jews during the Nazi period.[10] For many years East German Jews discreetly protested the school curriculum and the media coverage of Israel, both of which in their view led to anti-Semitic tendencies in East German youth.

The discussion of anti-Semitism in one of the earliest East German schoolbooks (1951) repeats an argument that had informed Marxist discourse during the war and which would continue to determine East German writing for the next 39 years.

> The Nazis twisted class conflicts into non-existing racial conflict. Racial persecution, the most backward, most reactionary point of view, was used by the Nazis as a "lightening rod" for the strong social tension. This is the same method used by American reactionaries against Negroes. (*Lehrbuch* 1951: 17)

East German textbooks had little room for psychological investigations into hatred of the Other:

> The persecution of the Jews had primarily economic causes. The Hitler Party, which had once lied to its supporters and voters that it would establish socialism, was in reality the Party that was paid by monopoly capitalists and that supported capitalist societal structures. Non-Jewish imperialists had no objections to the removal of competitors of Jewish heritage. (*Lehrbuch* 1951: 17–18)

A number of ideologically charged and historically debatable assumptions are presented here as facts: that anti-Semitism has primarily economic motives; that the Nazis were mere henchmen for German monopoly capitalists; that German capitalists supported Hitler to eliminate the competition of German-Jewish capitalists; and that German Jews were imperialists (who might have supported Nazi policy had it not been directed at them). Ulbricht is reported to have commented that the Nazi seizure of Jewish property merely saved East Germans the trouble (Goschler 102), and the "Lessons from the Trial Against the Slánský Conspiracy Center," an East German Stalinist tract from 1952 that "explains" the reasons for the show trial against Czech Communists, argues in the same fashion ("Lehren" 206).

The 1951 textbook draws a clear connection between the early anti-Jewish actions of the Nazis and Auschwitz: "The fascist terror against the Jewish people had begun with racial persecution and ended with the murder of millions of Jewish people in extermination camps. From 9.5 million Jews in Europe, about 5 million were murdered. Nazi racial persecution had an even more horrible effect on the Slavic peoples, on Poland and above all on the Soviet Union" (*Lehrbuch* 18). Hence Olaf Groehler's assertion that "the first schoolbooks of the GDR did not once mention the Holocaust" (GSA 4; "Umgang" 242) is only true from a narrowly semantic point of view, for the word "Holocaust" was not used in East Germany. As early as 1946 the first official *Richtlinien für den Unterricht* (Guidelines for Teaching) in the Soviet Occupation Zone contain references to the Jewish catastrophe, and in 1951 the first history schoolbook of the GDR speaks frankly of the extermination camps, although the imperatives of Soviet historiography are also clear with the emphasis on Slavic deaths. But it is true that the Soviets lost over 20 million citizens, and that the Poles lost 6 million (about half of whom were Jews).

The rhetorical slippage one finds in the formulations above becomes more pronounced with the discussions of slave labor and of the political and economic uses of the camps. Asserting that 5 million involuntary or slave workers were brought to Germany, the text declares that "armaments industrialists earned incredible profits from this exploitation" (*Lehrbuch* 1951: 52). Writing of the death camps, the authors charge: "German capitalists profited from this mass murder" (*Lehrbuch* 1951: 53). With the emphasis on the political-economic aspect of the camps, the singularity of Nazi anti-Semitism is subsumed in the formulations of the authors. Speaking of the concentration camps, they write:

> People hated by the Nazis died by the tens of thousands in these camps: professors, engineers, religious leaders, politicians, workers, Jews, French, Czechoslovakian citizens, Soviet soldiers and officers.
> In addition to the work camps there were extermination camps for the people who were supposed to be murdered immediately. In the infamous camp of Auschwitz a total of five million people were gassed and cremated. (*Lehrbuch* 1951: 53)

At the conclusion of the discussion of the Nazi camps, the text states simply that in the roughly 300 Nazi concentration camps "more than 11 million" died (*Lehrbuch* 1951: 53). Similar formulations will recur in East German schoolbooks for the next thirty-eight years. The omission of such victims as Sinti and Roma, homosexuals, Jehovah's Witnesses, the ill or handicapped, parallels West German depictions from the early 1950s.

In the edition of 1954 the rhetoric remains essentially unchanged. Discussing the Jewish tragedy the authors clearly state, as they had in 1951:

> The fascists murdered in their extermination camps approximately 5 million Jews, more than half of the Jewish population of Europe.
> In the war the Nazi racial persecution had a horrible effect on the Slavic peoples: on Poland and especially on the Soviet people.
> (*Lehrbuch* 1954: 201)

The only change from 1951 is the elimination of "even more" from the formulation "even more horrible effect." As in the 1951 edition, there is mention of the *Einsatztruppen* and of massacres of Jews in Kiev or Riga. But the final mention of the extermination camps again utilizes the circumlocutions of "people" and "11 million" (*Lehrbuch* 1954: 236).

The practice of listing the dead by profession or by nation was standard with orthodox Soviet and Polish historians, and was utilized, as we have noted, by the East German historian Walter Bartel in two texts from the mid-1950s that served as reference works for teachers of history in the GDR. In those two texts there is no mention of the ultimate number of Jews killed, and at telling moments the word "Jew" is not employed at all.

Neueste Zeit, the upper form East German schoolbook from 1958, follows Bartel's lead. The book describes the "idiocy" of the

Nuremberg Laws in greater detail than its predecessors (32–34). It contains pictures of persecuted Jews in Poland, and it describes the Warsaw Ghetto revolt. It also contains appendices displaying the report of an SS commander detailing the number of Jews and Communists his troops had murdered (about 40 to 1, respectively); describing the destruction of the Warsaw Ghetto; and containing the final letter of an unknown Jewish woman murdered by the Nazis in 1943. But the total number of Jews killed by the Nazis is nowhere to be found. Instead one finds circumlocutions similar to those we have seen in earlier East German schoolbooks (but without the accompanying final numbers): "[SS commandos] murdered millions of men, women, and children because they were ill or unable to work, because they were Jews or antifascists. In the gas chambers of the infamous concentration camp Oswiecim (Auschwitz) alone five million concentration camp prisoners met death. The poison gas for these deaths was delivered by IG Farben" (*Neueste Zeit* 1958: 97). The edition of *Neueste Zeit* from 1961 remains unchanged in this respect, as does the 1961 history textbook for the tenth class, although in this latter text the number of people murdered at Auschwitz drops to 2.5 million. The Polish people, the text notes, lost six million, a sixth of its population. The text does not indicate that three million were Jews (*Lehrbuch* 1961: 12). The Marxist economic argument plus the exigencies of Soviet historiography hence threatened, by the end of the first ten years of the GDR, to eliminate the Jewish Holocaust from East German schoolbooks.

This changed radically in the early 1960s, as the Eichmann trial concentrated the world's attention on Nazi crimes against Jews. In the 1963 printing (1960 edition) of a book for the ninth class, the authors speak of Nazi anti-Semitism and add:

> The Nazis raised this false doctrine into law. Those were the so-called Nuremberg Laws, for which Adenauer's current Secretary of State, Dr. Globke, wrote the interpretative commentary. Under the protection of him and other infamous anti-Semites, outrages against Jews are increasingly numerous today in West Germany, where the same fascist monster is coming back to life.
>
> (*Lehrbuch* 1963: 246)

This was followed by a description of the "*Kristallnacht*," after which the following sentence is restored: "During the period of their hegemony the fascists murdered in their extermination camps 6 million Jews, more than half of the Jewish population of Europe" (*Lehrbuch* 1963: 247).

The 1965 printing of a text for the tenth grade intensifies the campaign against West Germany:

> The extermination of the Jews took place on the basis of the Nuremberg Laws, whose co-author was Globke, for many years the closest advisor of the former West German Chancellor Adenauer. In different occupied countries he also personally introduced the extermination measures against the Jews. In the area of Lvov the terror took 700,000 victims. The "Nightingale" battalion, led by the former Bonn minister Oberländer, was especially active in such atrocities. (*Lehrbuch* 1965: 26)

The acknowledgment in earlier texts of racial persecution — to be sure, an acknowledgment coupled with the assurance that such persecution was but an ideological diversion — appears weakened: "[The fascists] murdered many millions of Jews, Poles, Russians, Ukrainians; above all people in whom they suspected political opponents" (*Lehrbuch* 1965: 26). As the racial receded behind the political, so it disappeared in the economic: "In some of the extermination camps the fascists had gas chambers built, in which many thousand men, women, and also children — even babies — died a tortured death. The poison gas for this mass murder was delivered by the IG-Farben cartel" (*Lehrbuch* 1965: 27–29). By 1965, the six million murdered Jews had again disappeared from the textbooks of East German schools. The text states simply: "In concentration camps alone 8 million people were murdered" (*Lehrbuch* 1965: 61).

The six million Jews do not reappear until 1984. They are not present in a 1969 printing, which notes only: "Poland lost six million people in the years of the fascist occupation; the majority were Jewish citizens" (*Lehrbuch* 241). In a 1976 printing the Jews are one category among many:

> Communists, antifascists, and those persecuted due to racial grounds, especially Jews, had a particularly difficult lot. They were held captive in concentration camps. In addition to prisoners from every European country there were hundreds of thousands of Soviet citizens. Over 8 million people of different nations and classes, above all [*in erster Linie*] workers, Communists, Soviet citizens, progressive members of the intelligentsia, and Jews, were brutally murdered in the camps. (*Geschichte* 1976: 206)

This last formulation recurs in the 1984 edition (1987 printing: 162) with the addition of Poles as a victim group. But by the 1980s East German historians had somewhat more leeway in describing the Jewish tragedy, which had again become state interest. In a box added to the description of the *"Kristallnacht,"* the important dates of the Jewish persecution are presented, including, in bold typeface, the "extermination of approximately six million Jews" (*Geschichte* 1987: 133). After a nineteen-year hiatus, the six-million figure had returned to East German schoolbooks, and it remained in those used between 1984 and 1990.

Proceeding from the tenets of Marxism-Leninism, East German historians occasionally attained important results. With the end of the Cold War, historians in a unified Germany may be more ready to reexamine East German investigations into the role of German capitalism in Hitler's rise to power, or the economic uses of the camps with their slave labor, or the effects of millions of foreign workers in the German war economy. East German historians researched the Communist resistance to Hitler, and they never forgot the millions of Soviet POWs murdered in Nazi camps (Ministerium 226), or that Slavs in general died by the millions. They also investigated the crucial role of the Red Army in Hitler's defeat. The US historian Konrad Jarausch asserts that the technical quality of East German historical research improved during the 1970s and 1980s; the results of that research could sometimes serve as a valuable corrective to work done in the West (94).

Nonetheless, as Groehler points out, East German historians could never spring over their own shadow, and they never seriously questioned the dogma of the Comintern fascism definition ("Umgang" 243). In 1976 Konrad Kwiet had asserted that "no major contribution to our real understanding of German-Jewish history has hitherto come out of the GDR" (198). Over 15 years later, Groehler wrote that by international standards — and also given the East German self-definition as an antifascist state — too little was accomplished.[11] East German historiography was "defined through political encrustation and instrumentalization, and unconventional research ideas were nipped in the bud or stifled. The uniqueness of the Holocaust was never recognized and hence trivialized. Above all, a decisive dimension of the discussion regarding the persecution of the Jews and the Holocaust was never put into question but rather was carefully and systematically derailed: the personal confrontation of every citizen in the GDR with the persecution and murder of the Jews" (Groehler, "Holocaust" 62). Jarausch notes that state supervision dictated research agendas, while implicit and explicit censorship deformed them (91). Dogma frequently collided with facts or outran them (e.g., the role of capitalism in Hitler's rise has been difficult to document [Jarausch 89–90]). The strident partisanship of East German historians also proved repugnant to most independent scholars, who often not incorrectly viewed such historiography as affirmative if not propagandistic. Rainer Eckert cites one East German historian whose statement from 1980 has exemplary character: "Anyone who undertakes scholarly research on fascism is aware of the fact that he is not dealing with a historically concluded theme, but is directly involved in the class struggle of our time" (Cited in Eckert, "Ende" 88).

The German-Israeli political scientist Dan Diner has pointed out that it was ultimately more through antifascism than through socialism that the GDR attempted to legitimate itself as a civic culture and an independent state (127). East German historians had a special role in this: they were at once "guardians of the moral flame" (Jarausch 85) and the first line of defense (Diner 129). The propagandistic results of the historians' project should not be underestimated, as Diner, Ulrich Herbert, and others point out. For many leftists in the West, the GDR, despite Stalinist deformations, counted as the better Germany. And indeed, the East German insistence that anti-Semitism was used to divert attention from class issues is hardly preposterous, nor is the emphasis on class struggle and contemporary forms of fascism. But ultimately the tone of moral outrage affected by so many East German historians rang hollow. They could not credibly lambaste "resurgent anti-Semitism" in the Federal Republic while ignoring the continuation of fascist thought patterns in the GDR (Maaz), the structural similarities of Nazism and Stalinism, or East bloc state-sponsored anti-Semitism. Such hypocrisy was apparent to East German citizens as well, and it undermined their historians and the state's first line of defense. Whether it is also true, as Jarausch asserts, that the insistence on economic reductionism "did not engage the racial dimension of anti-Semitism and insufficiently inoculated youth against xenophobia" (94), remains an open question.[12]

Notes

[1] "Holocaust" 54. See Kurt Gossweiler's vehement dementi of this and other assertions by Groehler.

[2] Groehler, "Juden" 51. For more on Merker, see Herf.

[3] I do not mean this with regard to the term "Holocaust" itself, which has only gained acceptance fairly recently and which was hardly used in the GDR even in the 1980s. I mean rather that the Nazi genocide of the Jews is not explicitly discussed in East German history writing from the 1950s.

[4] Bartel, *Deutschland* 178. See also the virtually identical wording in the book version of 1956.

[5] Bartel was "purged" after the war, and his academic career represented a demotion from his previous position as head of President Pieck's office. Nonetheless, the SED stylized him into an essential element in what has been called its "foundation myth." See Niethammer, esp. 129-133.

[6] See also the introduction to the East German translation of the Polish collection of documents *Faschismus - Getto - Massenmord*, published in 1960: "May no reader put this book down with the remark that the horrible events depicted here belong fortunately to the past and are only of interest in that way. The most recent anti-Semitic outbursts in West Germany teach us otherwise" (Jüdisches 5).

[7] The Holocaust did not figure prominently in East German history writing from the 1950s, but it was present in East German discourse in other ways. Discussions appeared in schoolbooks, literary works (e.g., Hermlin's "Die Zeit der Gemeinsamkeit"), and film (e.g., Wolf's *Sterne*). The stage version of Anne Frank's diary also played in the GDR.

[8] Eschwege, *Kennzeichen* 10. For the most thorough response to such allegations, see Turner.

[9] For a comparison of East and West German schoolbooks, see Uhe.

[10] Kirchner, "Die jüdische" 33. The Nazi period was also covered in literature classes with Friedrich Wolf's play *Professor Mamlock* (1934) and Bruno Apitz's novel *Nackt unter Wölfen* (1958). For more on those works, see chapter 4.

[11] For a more optimistic East German view, published before the end of the GDR, see Schmidt.

[12] See for example Chapter 3, note 21.

2: The Texture of Memory: East German Concentration Camp Memorials

> *For too often a community's monuments assume the polished, finished veneer of a death mask, unreflective of current memory, unresponsive to contemporary issues.*
>
> James Young

In *Imagined Communities*, Benedict Anderson writes:

No more arresting emblems of the modern culture of nationalism exist than cenotaphs and tombs of Unknown Soldiers . . . . The cultural significance of such monuments becomes even clearer if one tries to imagine, say, a Tomb of the Unknown Marxist or a cenotaph for fallen Liberals. Is a sense of absurdity avoidable? The reason is that neither Marxism nor Liberalism are much concerned with death and immortality. If the nationalist imagining is so concerned, this suggests a strong affinity with religious imaginings.

(9–10)

Yet East Germany featured, in a sense, Tombs of Unknown Marxists. In Schinkel's *Neue Wache* on the central boulevard in East Berlin, and at the Buchenwald concentration camp memorial — two sites constitutive in the construction of an East German national identity — the state erected monuments containing the remains of unknown antifascist resistance fighters killed by the Nazis. In its attempt to define itself against capitalist, prosperous West Germany, East Germany, with its questionable economy and unpopular government, advertised itself more as a German antifascist state than as a socialist one That nationalist imagining indeed featured a religious component.

The East German antifascist concentration camp memorials functioned, a historian at Buchenwald told me, as the "churches of socialism." His characterization appears entirely appropriate. On the sacred ground of those sites, the congregation would meet for ritual ceremonies and communion, solemnly commemorating the martyrs who had been sacrificed for the socialist future. The *Jugendweihe*, a secularized confirmation for East German children, regularly occurred at the former camps. The Sachsenhausen memorial camp contained a speaker's podium that, as a German historical commission noted, resembled an altar (Ministerium 236). The East German antifascist memorial at Buchenwald appeals unabashedly to Christian symbolism, elevating the murdered KPD leader Ernst Thälmann to a prophet or even Christ figure. The visitor to the Buchenwald bell tower is invited to proceed on a journey that metaphorically parallels that of the German Communist Party in this century, at least in that Party's self-image: descent into Hell, followed by purgation and salvation.[1]

As with the required schoolbooks previously discussed, these sites provided the East German government an irresistible opportunity to propagate its view of history, one replete, as we have seen, with gaps and half-truths. The government tailored the camps to educate its citizenry to a point of view, and the sites furthermore served as international propaganda for the East German antifascist program. In this latter point, at least, the SED achieved some success. The western German historian Ulrich Herbert noted in 1992 that German unification brought to the surface international fears of resurgent German militarism, nationalism, and racism, but that such reservations were invariably directed at West, not East Germany ("Zweierlei" 9).

An essay published in 1988 by Ottomar Rothmann, an East German who worked in the Buchenwald camp museum, illustrates concisely the pedagogical tasks of the camps. Since Buchenwald was opened as a museum in 1958 some 12 million visitors from almost every country had visited.[2] Of the approximately 400,000 visitors per year, approximately 120,000 were East German youths, who were a primary target of the educational efforts (128). According to Rothmann, the overriding purpose of the camp exhibitions was to transmit the legacy of the resistance struggle against the German fascists (127). In this task, he added proudly, the museum worked closely with the antifascist SED (127–28).

Rothmann noted that among the additional goals of his memorial site was the illustration of the role monopoly capital played in the rise of Hitler; the demonstration of the guilt of the ruling classes (many East German youth "still have unclear ideas about the class situation of that time" when they first visit the camps [129]); and an emphasis on the decisive role of the Communist resistance (128–

29). The museum especially attempted to direct attention to the role models, the antifascist fighters who had been able to attain the "correct" point of view (130).

The memorial sites were not merely interested in purveying "history," Rothmann emphasized repeatedly, but rather the continuity between past and present. (He himself managed to work in an oblique attack on the US development of the Strategic Defense Initiative [130]). The camps were especially useful for this type of work, "because at the actual locations of the event one can create a strong emotional effect, especially on the youthful visitors" (130).

The East Germans maintained three "National Warning and Memorial Sites." Buchenwald, outside of Weimar in the south of the former GDR, opened in 1958. Ravensbrück, a former women's camp located in Fürstenberg/Havel, north of Berlin, was opened as a memorial site in 1959, and Sachsenhausen, located in the Berlin suburb of Oranienburg, in 1961.[3] (A fourth memorial opened in 1988 in Brandenburg, where Party Chief Erich Honecker had been imprisoned during the Third Reich). The museums were similar in construction and approach, an approach outlined in a special statute passed in 1961. According to this law (passed, curiously enough, after all three memorials were already in operation) the sites were to demonstrate:

a) the struggle of the German working class and of all democratic forces against the fascist threat;
b) the role of the KPD as the strongest and leading force in the struggle against the criminal Nazi regime;
c) the antifascist resistance in the years between 1933 and 1945 in Germany and the European countries;
d) the SS-terror in the camps and the lack of respect for human life;
e) the common struggle of the members of European nations, especially the Soviet POWs, against the SS-terror, and the special role of international solidarity in this fight as well as the measures that led to the liberation of the camps;
f) the resurrection of fascism and militarism in West Germany;
g) the historical role of the GDR (Ministerium 223).

Ottomar Rothmann was just following orders: his essay adhered rather closely to the prescriptions outlined in this statute. The statute also makes clear that what Rothmann terms the educational mission was in fact a clearly intentioned instrumentalization of history. The victims themselves (especially if they did not attain the "correct" viewpoint) receive little attention — but one category, letter "d," among seven. In the following I examine more closely some of the tropes of instrumentalization in East German memorials to the victims of National Socialism: the celebration of the Soviet Union and the KPD; the interpretation of Nazism; the efforts to establish parallels with the present; and the discussion of Jewish victims. I conclude with a glance at the controversies surrounding the sites after the opening of the Wall in 1989.

Celebration of the Soviet Union

As is well known, the German army invaded the Soviet Union in June 1941. The Germans committed unspeakable atrocities against Soviet citizens, especially but not only the Jews, and the Soviets lost over 20 million citizens during the war. The German defeat at Stalingrad was celebrated in East German historiography as the turning point in the war, as the battle that broke Hitler's neck. The East German concentration camp museums constantly emphasized fascist savagery and Soviet sacrifices (and the fact that Soviet soldiers liberated Sachsenhausen and Ravensbrück) to justify the continuing Soviet military occupation and, indirectly, the repressive SED government.

A Soviet tank stands at the entrance to Ravensbrück, with a weathered sign proclaiming glory and honor to the Soviets. The tank of course symbolized the Soviet liberation of Ravensbrück, but for East German citizens it also served as a reminder that the Red Army was willing to use force — as it did in the GDR in 1953, Hungary in 1956, or Czechoslovakia in 1968 — to maintain its power. Soviet military might was well in evidence at the camps, and not merely in the manner of, say, Sachsenhausen's socialist realist sculpture of a towering Soviet soldier holding his cape protectively over two liberated prisoners. In Fürstenberg, a small resort town where thirty thousand Soviet soldiers far outnumbered the population of about five thousand Germans, the military occupied almost the entire former Ravensbrück camp, and the museum was relegated to a smallish area on the fringe. To enter the latter memorial, one walked through part of the barracks, with a picturesque lake on one side and former SS houses, now shabby, boarded up, or used by the Soviets, on the other. In Buchenwald the Soviet barracks was located between the memorial and the city, and the woods between the barracks and the camp were used for military maneuvers. In Sachsenhausen, part of the former camp served as a Soviet, and later East German military barracks. East German tanks used fields containing mass graves as a practice site.

The Soviet exhibition at Ravensbrück consisted of pictures illustrating the numerous atrocities committed by the Germans during their occupation of parts of the Soviet Union. (The Soviet exhibit in Auschwitz was very similar in form and content). In the Sachsenhausen camp museum a socialist realist sketch demonstrated the solidarity of the camp's organized political prisoners (organized of course by the Communists, especially German Communists) who smuggled bread to Soviet POWs.[4] One could read that the "most horrible of the crimes committed by the SS in the nine years of Sachsenhausen was the murder of over 18,000 Soviet prisoners of war in the period from the beginning of September to the middle of November 1941." A monument in the ruins of that camp's gas chamber commemorates, with language similar to that of the tank at Ravensbrück, the Soviets, and only them: "Glory and Honor to the Fallen Heroes." In Sachsenhausen's second museum, the Museum of the Antifascist Resistance Struggle of the European Peoples, European countries were allotted fifty square meters of exhibition space, although the Soviet exhibition (as well as that celebrating "The Other [i.e., antifascist] Germany") received one hundred. The latter two exhibitions led the visitor visually to a large photograph of the towering Soviet war memorial in Berlin-Treptow.

The art of Sachsenhausen also attempted to elicit pro-Soviet sentiment, whether through Walter Womacka's pathos-laden stained glass windows in the European Resistance museum or with René Graetz's sculpture of the Soviet soldier holding his cape protectively around two inmates.[5] Behind the grouping is a forty-meter obelisk with the names of countries that lost citizens in Sachsenhausen; the obelisk makes clear the need for international resistance, led by the Soviet Union, to fascism. East German architects altered the structure of the camp in order to focus attention on the monument by creating a wall around the parade ground, thus blocking the view of the original topography of terror. The wall features an opening that leads visually and physically to the domineering obelisk.

In Buchenwald a shrine in a cell block commemorated nine Soviet prisoners murdered during an SS massacre in the night of 9–10

April 1945. A plaque noted that Soviet prisoners were "decisively involved" in the organization of resistance within the camp, that thousands fell for their fatherland and for those oppressed by fascism, and that the SS turned its hatred especially against the Soviet prisoners. An engraved stone marking the spot of one of the six barracks housing Soviet prisoners notes that "in scorn of all international law, Soviet soldiers were held prisoner in Buchenwald. In addition to performing the heaviest work they were brutally tortured, and many died of exhaustion and hunger despite solidarity from political prisoners."[6] A similar stone marks the location, somewhat removed from the main camp, of the *Genickschußanlage*, a building disguised as a medical examination station in which prisoners were shot in the back of the neck or head while standing on what they thought was a scale: "Against all international law, hundreds of thousands of Soviet prisoners of war were brought into the concentration camps and were murdered. On this spot 8,483 soldiers and officers suffered a violent death. They fought and died as heroes of their socialist fatherland for the liberation of humanity from fascism." This site was, however, not regularly visited, and a reconstructed *Genickschußanlage* stands in the main camp enclosure with a similar plaque. In the event that one had nonetheless missed the information, it was repeated in the museum: "Against the norms of international military law the Soviet prisoners were subjected to especially inhumane conditions." The number of deaths in the *Genickschußanlage* was again mentioned, as was, elsewhere in the museum, the poor rations of the Soviet prisoners. But the attempt of the fascists to conquer the Soviet Union failed, we learned, due to the "superiority of the socialist state and social order."

There is no doubt that the pro-Soviet propaganda that informed East German life, and which was particularly pronounced at the concentration camp memorials, had the desired effect on many citizens, especially in the intelligentsia. Burdened by the guilt of German war crimes, convinced that capitalism bore the responsibility for those crimes and that the Federal Republic hence provided no alternative, East German intellectuals were willing to overlook a pervasive repression in light of the "greater danger" looming in the West. In this they were very different from their colleagues in, for example, Poland or Czechoslovakia. Furthermore, East German intellectuals, despite their rhetoric celebrating the common man, fundamentally mistrusted him, for they knew of what barbarism the Germans had

been capable. They also knew, although the subject remained a taboo in historical writing, how susceptible the German working class
had been to the Nazi movement. Although rarely expressed so
openly, these arguments remained, for many, cogent reasons for an
"educational" dictatorship, that is, one that guided East German
citizens to enlightenment.

In the collective memory of the majority of the population, however, a different situation obtained. East Germans *knew* of German
crimes in the East, but they had *experienced* the war at home. Many
had witnessed the destruction of German cities by allied bombs (on
reconstructed buildings of architectural merit the SED government
rarely missed the opportunity to point out that the destruction had
come from Anglo-American bombers); many had also experienced
the rape and pillage that occurred during the allied invasion, especially in areas under Soviet control.[7] These people felt themselves to
be victims of the war. (The East German writer Christa Wolf presents just such a person in a cameo portrait of an East Berlin taxi
driver in *Kindheitsmuster* [Patterns of Childhood, 1976]).

The East German population also carried in its unwritten historical memory the knowledge that between 1945 and 1950 the Soviets
had used Sachsenhausen and Buchenwald, as well as other sites, as
special internment camps. Thousands of Germans were imprisoned
in the camps and many were sent from there to the Soviet Union as
laborers. Numerous detainees were guilty of Nazi crimes, but some
had been youthful "Werewolves," and some had committed no
crime whatsoever. The Soviets and their German Communist allies
also used the camps to further their Cold War purposes by impris-
oning political opponents, including Social Democrats. Many of
those detainees had themselves opposed the Nazis; some had been
prisoners in the same camps in which they found themselves after
1945. Of the thousands of Germans who were "disappeared" into
the camps, many never returned, and after 1989, mass graves were
uncovered outside some of the former Soviet detention centers.
Outside Sachsenhausen, for example, an estimated 15,000–30,000
dead lie in such graves.[8] The insistent pro-Soviet celebrations in the
camps hence rang hollow for many East Germans. The aggressive
pathos combined with an equally aggressive suppression of other
historical viewpoints led ultimately to a trivialization of the stagger-
ing Soviet sacrifices in the Second World War. The Red Army tank
at the entrance to Ravensbrück, today standing bereft of the former

flags on a shoddy, overgrown square, serves for many Germans as an object of scorn and ridicule.

Celebration of the German Communist Party and Other Communist Parties

Closely linked with the glorification of the Soviet Union was the assertion of the leading role of the KPD during the 1930s and 1940s. The KPD, as the introductory movie at Buchenwald insisted, repeatedly warned the German people about Hitler. Outlawed, it organized and led political resistance as an underground organization both in and outside the camps. Camp memorials (as well as the East German exhibition at Auschwitz) emphasized the martyrdom of the German Communist resistance fighters. Only in the exhibition after 1989 could historians mention that the strict organization of the Communists helped them survive, but at the cost of other groups whom the Communists substituted for their comrades during "selections." Compared with other groups of victims, the numbers of Communist martyrs, at least at Buchenwald, was small.

Resistance was generally defined as political, with Communist leadership; other forms or groups received secondary mention or were ignored entirely. (A literary example is Bruno Apitz's *Nackt unter Wölfen* [Naked among Wolves, 1958], which only mentions Communists in the Buchenwald resistance organization, although Eugen Kogon's *Der SS-Staat* [The SS State, 1947] lists non-Communists who were involved). Some members of the 20 July assassination attempt on Hitler were held in isolation cells at Buchenwald, but because those plotters were celebrated in the Federal Republic and were largely ignored in the GDR, the East German government tore down the isolation cells and did not mention the internment of those prisoners (Monteath 7) — a striking example of the fashion in which the construction (or destruction) of memory can be physically shaped. The 20 July assassination plot also did not figure in the Sachsenhausen European Resistance museum.

In Ravensbrück an exhibit declared that "Ravensbrück was the venue for a heroic resistance struggle against the atrocities and terror of the Nazis. Initiators of the antifascist struggle and the organized resistance were the Communists." In Sachsenhausen one read that "the Communists, educated by their Party to be selfless fighters, organized and led the struggle." In Buchenwald, which due to the myth of a Communist-led self-liberation was the showcase East German memorial camp (regarding the self-liberation, one need only read speeches from 1946 — before the instrumentalization of the camps commenced — in which the US Army is thanked for the liberation [Knigge 69]), the celebration of Communist-led resistance was especially pronounced. James Young writes that "the Buchenwald National Memorial, the most gargantuan complex of memorial sculptures and edifices located at any of the German camps, is striking for its largely triumphal scenes of uprising and self-liberation. In the sheer size of the sculpture and by virtue of the spectacular landscape, the state hoped to monumentalize beyond question its own reason for being, to create a site that would remember definitively the state's own birth."[9] The three memorial sites also emphasized — at times in a manner bordering on the condescending — the fashion in which Communists aided children, British POWs, Jews, or Sinti and Roma. The latter entered Buchenwald "without political experience" and were hence "helpless"; without Communist assistance they would have perished in even greater numbers. Implied here is the attitude one sometimes found between the lines of East German historiography: in a sense, the Jews or Sinti and Roma had themselves to blame for their genocide, since they did not, as Ottomar Rothmann expressed it, find their way to the correct point of view and work with the KPD.

The concentration camp memorials also emphasized the special suffering of the left. Ernst Heilmann, the leading Prussian Social Democrat, died after "frightful torture," and the Communist organizer Rudolph Opitz was "martyred" "especially cruelly." At the entrance to the Sachsenhausen camp museum visitors learned that "the majority of the political prisoners were Communists. *Especially against them* was directed the ghastly terror to which many of the best and leading comrades succumbed" (my emphasis). In the Buchenwald museum one read that the "fury of the SS directed itself *above all* against German Communists in camp functions" (my emphasis).

The most celebrated martyr was Ernst Thälmann, chair of the KPD. Arrested shortly after the Nazis seized power, Thälmann was held for eleven years in Buchenwald, where he was murdered on 18 August 1944. The site of his death was marked at Buchenwald with a plaque and flowers, and elsewhere in the camp the SED set up what can best be termed a shrine to his memory. Throughout the former GDR, evidence of the Thälmann cult of personality existed: biographies of Thälmann written by East German President Wilhelm Pieck or Party Chief Walter Ulbricht were widely available; a statue of Thälmann stands near the train station in Weimar; a large park was named after him in East Berlin; organized youth groups were called Thälmann Pioneers; a poem glorifying Thälmann concluded the camp museum exhibition at Sachsenhausen; large photographs of him superimposed on the masses were central to Sachsenhausen's European Resistance museum; and a poem by Johannes R. Becher associates Thälmann with Christ and is inscribed on the pylons at the Buchenwald bell tower. Yet according to the western German newsmagazine *Der Spiegel*, the KPD and the Soviet Union wanted a martyr and made no attempt to free the increasingly bitter and disillusioned leader (29 July 1996).

Through its constant incantation of Communist leadership and martyrdom, the SED sought a moral and political space for its continued leadership (dictatorship) in East Germany. The repeated references, both in the camps and in such books as those by historian Heinz Kühnrich, to the fact that the KPD had warned the Germans, and that the people did not listen, served to illustrate the wisdom of the Party and the fundamental immaturity of the masses. The Communists *were* the best organized political resistance group both inside and outside the camps. As with the Soviets, however, they squandered what political capital they possessed after the war by suppressing other voices. In 1993 the director of the Sachsenhausen camp called it one of the worst-researched of the former Nazi camps (*taz* 26 June 1993). The Sachsenhausen archives maintained only 1,600 reports from former prisoners, most written during the 1970s and 90% from political prisoners. But 90% of the roughly 200,000 detainees at Sachsenhausen were *not* political prisoners, an impression one would not have received had one visited the camp during GDR times. At the center of the memorial site stands the soaring obelisk displaying red triangles and only red triangles — the badge of the political prisoner. Similarly, the wall decorating the grave of the Unknown Antifascist Resistance Fighter at Buchenwald featured only red triangles, as did the numerous memorials, dotting the East German landscape, commemorating the death marches of 1944–45. In 1990, after the collapse of the dictatorship but in the "Yet-GDR," the final room of the Sachsenhausen camp museum was provisionally changed. A simple exhibition showed badges of all colors

and contained the single sentence: "To all the victims of Sachsenhausen."

Hitler and the Capitalists

In his 1988 essay describing pedagogical work at the concentration
camp memorials, Ottomar Rothmann wrote that East German
schoolchildren who first visited the sites often possessed unclear
ideas about economic relations in the 1920s and 1930s. The museum exhibitions and supporting materials were clearly designed to
help children to the correct point of view, the Comintern or Dimitrov theory. At the outset of the Buchenwald museum the explanatory signs noted that the fascist program corresponded to the interests of the most reactionary and chauvinist circles of monopoly
capitalism, a point repeated in the introductory film and in the brochure that served as a guide to the museum. The first sentence in
Kreuzweg Ravensbrück (Ravensbrück: The Way to the Cross,
1987),[10] a book containing short essays on the lives of 17 Ravensbrück inmates, asserts that "on 30 January 1933 the most aggressive
powers of the German monopoly capitalist bourgeoisie transferred
power to the fascists in Germany" (Jacobeit 10). In Sachsenhausen
and Ravensbrück the Dimitrov doctrine was reduced to a simple
pictorial equation. Photographs of leading German industrialists carried the caption: "The Taskmasters." Beneath them hung pictures of
important Nazis with the caption: "The Henchmen."

The East German museums argued that big business brought
Hitler to power and that the camps served German business as a
convenient source of slave labor. Hence at the beginning of the
Sachsenhausen camp museum visitors read in large letters that "The
armaments industry squeezed the last ounce out of the inmates."
The Sachsenhausen European Resistance museum opened with the
Comintern definition and with artist John Heartfield's collage depiction of Hitler as a capitalist marionette. The museums devoted
considerable attention to the various businesses that utilized camp
labor, such as Siemens in Ravensbrück or I. G. Farben in Sachsenhausen. The Sachsenhausen camp museum displayed an enlarged
statistical table from a Heinz Kühnrich book, a table which in the
book is unattributed, detailing the profit that could be made from a
prisoner. Outside the barracks where Buchenwald SS doctors conducted their brutal experiments, a sign explained that such experi-

ments "brought the German monopoly leaders millions in profits." In the Buchenwald brochure the author summarized: "The millions which German big business once invested in Hitler came to rich fruition" (Ritscher 24).

The concentration camp memorials set in stone the tenets of East German historiography, including its weaknesses. Thus the Buchenwald brochure asserted that as of 1942 the "fascist state could no longer afford to murder masses of prisoners or to let them simply perish" (Ritscher 24). Yet at that point the "Final Solution" was already in operation, regardless of economic or strategic consequences. The economic benefits provided by slave laborers also proved marginal, as even the East German historians Goguel and Pätzold admitted, but that is not the impression one received from the camp museums, which spoke of windfall profits. The profits did not all go to German industrialists, either; the SS built a large and in some ways competing economic empire. The Gustloff armaments factory at Buchenwald, to name one example, was SS-owned and operated. And, finally, the fact that German industry profited from the camps, repugnant though it is, does not prove that German big business brought Hitler to power.

Still, German industry *did* profit from the camps, and many firms participated in the Nazi program of extinction through work. Companies with branches at the concentration or extermination camps — Krupp or Siemens, for example — continued profitably in West Germany after the war, sometimes with the same personnel. Some firms never paid restitution, others did so reluctantly. The Nazis furthermore imported over seven and a half million foreign workers to work throughout Germany, often in degrading or inhuman conditions.[11] West German camp memorials sometimes had difficulty with these facts, which were underplayed as much as they were overplayed in the East. It will be of interest to watch how this aspect of German history is portrayed in the concentration camp memorials of the new Germany.

The Past Present

The East German emphasis on industrial exploitation and profit in the camps served to demonstrate that the past was not dead, that it lived on — if not in the GDR, then in the Federal Republic, where Siemens and other companies thrived. The insecure and inferior

GDR needed desperately to differentiate itself from powerful West Germany, and the concentration camps proved extremely useful in that regard. In a sense, the camps provided the GDR its raison d'être.

If capitalism had brought the Nazis to power, then — so argued the East Germans — only a break with capitalism could guarantee freedom from such horrors. The Federal Republic remained capitalist, the East Germans never failed to emphasize, and hence a haven for past Nazis as well as a breeding ground for new ones. In the Buchenwald brochure the author admits that a US military tribune sentenced and executed Hermann Pister, Buchenwald Kommandant from 1942–45, but adds: "However, many other SS beasts from Buchenwald escaped punishment in the Western Zone of Occupation or the FRG or only had to serve short sentences" (Ritscher 3). He charges that although the murderers of Ernst Thälmann were found to be living in the Federal Republic in 1964, it took twenty-four years for a West German court to convict Wolfgang Otto, by then the only alleged perpetrator left alive (Ritscher 9). The GDR also attempted to emphasize differences between itself and the Federal Republic by christening the camp museums "national" warning and memorial sites; these "churches" were temples of (mostly German) Communist antifascist resistance and hence restricted to the GDR.

The constant emphasis on the leading role of the KPD in the resistance, and on Communist martyrdom in the camps, of course served as an attempt to legitimate the Communist dictatorship. Signs throughout the former GDR (a plaque at the Oranienburg train station has since been removed) marked the routes of various death marches that occurred when, near the end of the Second World War, the camps were evacuated to flee the approaching allies. The markers, which feature red triangles only, generally carry the assurance that the "legacy" of those prisoners lives on in our deeds, a cliché one finds on most East German antifascist monuments.

At the entrance to Ravensbrück a quote from Anna Seghers, written for children and hence infantilizing the visitor, commemorates the prisoners: "They are mothers and sisters of us all. You would not be able to learn or play freely, indeed, you would perhaps not be born, if such women had not placed their tender, delicate bodies like steel protection shields in front of you and your future during the entire period of the fascist dictatorship." Among other things, the quote implies that these "antifascist resistance fighters," and not the allies, were somehow responsible for Hitler's defeat and for the subsequent GDR. In the Sachsenhausen camp museum a large plaque proclaimed that if Communists were let out of the camp, "they rejoined the resistance movement. They shied away from no sacrifice, they did not fear death and they fell for a new, better Germany." The exhibit ended with a Brecht poem proclaiming these people to be "the true leaders of Germany." Two additional rooms then compared the achievements of East Germany with Globke's Germany. At Sachsenhausen's European Resistance museum the exhibition on German opposition to Hitler also culminated in the GDR, which included itself there among both victims and victors. Implicitly and explicitly, the museums argued relentlessly for the necessity of East Germany. In Buchenwald a memorial to the Social Democrat Ernst Heilmann contained an apologia for the Socialist Unity Party, the ruling Party in the GDR: "His death reminds us over and again of the important lesson: Fascism can only come to power when the working class is split."

Ultimately, the emphasis on the term "fascist" served to deemphasize the German element in a way that the specifically German terms "Nazi" or "National Socialist" would not. In the camp museums, the exhibits constantly differentiated between German or Hitler fascists (generally demonized — and hence distanced — as "beasts" or "monsters") and German antifascists, suggesting that the Hitler period constituted a kind of civil war. The same kind of logic allowed the East Germans to set up an exhibition among those of other victim nations at Auschwitz.

The de-Germanification of the camps also permitted the East Germans to argue, again in keeping with the Dimitrov theory, that fascism was a much larger concept than Hitler (or Mussolini). Outfitted with its antifascist credentials, the GDR displayed no embarrassment pillorying the "fascist" politics of Israel or arming the PLO. The regular ceremonies at the Buchenwald bell tower served as occasions to condemn the "fascist" politics of, say, the United States in Korea, Greece, Vietnam, or Chile, and the Sachsenhausen European Resistance museum transmitted the same message. A montage at the conclusion of the Buchenwald film bracketed an atomic explosion (we are to think, of course, of the USA) with a gathering at the Buchenwald bell tower and an image of the German cultural icons, Goethe and Schiller, in front of the National Theater in Weimar.

Remembering Jewish Victims

In the Buchenwald brochure the section explaining the Nazi concentration camp system concluded: "The German fascists imprisoned 18 million people from every European country in concentration camps. 11 million died in them" (Ritscher 22). With this verbal construct, one already familiar to us from East German schoolbooks, the six million Jews merge without mention with Hitler's other victims. Such formulations were not unusual. In a speech held in 1993 at Buchenwald, western German intellectual Wilfried Schoeller noted that "it belongs to history writing with blinders that the high percentage of Jewish prisoners at Buchenwald almost always remained unexamined; in the past one spoke almost always of a political camp" (*Frankfurter Rundschau* 15 April 1993). The eastern German historian Harry Stein admitted: "In the texture of memory of the victims of the concentration camp Buchenwald the fate of the Jews occupied over decades a tiny place. Yet early on — 1946 in Eugen Kogon's book — there was the indication that the history of Jewish prisoners in the camps deserved special attention and more space" (5). The East German camp memorials de-emphasized Jewish martyrdom, and as Stein writes, that was not "simply an oversight, but rather done with a purpose (*interessengeleitet*)" (5). Yet it is not true, as Claudia Koonz ("Germany's" 92) and others claim, that the Holocaust had no place at such memorials, or that the GDR suppressed all mention of Jews. Such misconceptions led the American journalist Charles Hoffman, for example, to the erroneous assumption that the exhibition in the Jewish barracks at Sachsenhausen was of recent origin (184). Within East German discourse the commemoration of Jewish victims had a purpose and a place, but only within limits implicitly or explicitly set by the Party.

In Buchenwald a memorial stone carries the following inscription in German, Russian, and Hebrew:[12] "Between November 1938 and February 1939 approximately 10,000 Jews — boys, men, old men — were imprisoned here. 600 of them were murdered in bestial fashion during this time. They died as victims of the fascist racial insanity." The Buchenwald museum contained several small exhibits documenting Jewish suffering, although those mentioned were invariably overshadowed by the emphasis on Communist martyrdom. In Sachsenhausen a separate barracks contained a small "Museum of the Resistance Struggle and the Suffering of Jewish Citizens."

At the beginning of the Buchenwald museum a display entitled *"Kristallnacht*. Persecution of Jewish Citizens" explained:

> Racism served German fascism as a veiling of social oppositions and as the means to incite the masses for its aggressive plans. Brutal disregard for the humanity of the Jews, mistreatment, mass persecutions, the destruction of their means of existence, and finally their expulsion from Germany formed one of the most disgusting chapters of fascist rule in Germany. It was the beginning of the systematic expulsion and massive murder of the Jewish population and of other, ostensibly racially inferior peoples from the areas occupied at times by the fascists in the Second World War.

This poster did not ignore the extermination of the Jews and others, but it did refrain from giving any numbers, either of the "Final Solution" or of Buchenwald in general. Indeed, the Buchenwald numbers under the SED are misleading: the memorial stone mentions 600 deaths, and in the museum exhibit there was an account of the murder of 21 Jews. Yet between 1937 and 1942 an estimated 2,795 Jews were murdered in Buchenwald, and in 11 months between 1944 and 1945, during the last phase of the "Final Solution," over 8,000 more were murdered (Stein 5). The SED exhibitions nowhere cited these numbers. The numbers for Sachsenhausen were first included in an exhibition set up after 1989 for a visit by Israeli Prime Minister Yitzhak Rabin.

The Buchenwald explanation of Nazi genocide practices derived from the standard Communist explanation that capitalists used Jews as a scapegoat to divert the workers from their true oppressors. This theory relegates anti-Semitism to the status of a secondary contradiction, one subordinate to class struggle, and the camp museums — like the structures of East German historiography — reflect that. In the Sachsenhausen Jewish museum a facsimile of the *Rote Fahne* (Red Flag), the KPD newspaper, depicted the KPD condemnation of the 1938 November pogrom and, similar to the poster displayed at Buchenwald, outlined the Communist theory of anti-Semitism. As with East German historiography, the concentration camp exhibitions nowhere indicated what Jeffrey Herf has ascertained: the *Rote Fahne* "statement was unique in the history of German Communism. Never, before or afterward, did the Central Committee of the KPD, or later the SED, give the Jewish question such a central role in the resistance to the Nazis, or so forcefully proclaim its solidarity with the Jews" ("German Communism" 264).

The Sachsenhausen Jewish museum provided a paradigmatic example of the East German instrumentalization of the Holocaust. In the early and mid-1950s there had been discussion of including a Jewish exhibition in a future Sachsenhausen memorial, but the idea was dropped. When representatives of the Institute for Marxism-Leninism and of the Museum for German History met in 1958 to plan the Sachsenhausen memorial, no separate Jewish exhibition was envisioned. In 1960 and 1961, the government and citizens of Israel complained that the recently opened East German Buchenwald memorial had misrepresented Jewish suffering; among other things, the Israelis objected to the fact that their country was not included in the Buchenwald Street of Nations, which contains monuments to (some) countries with citizens who were murdered at Buchenwald. When the East Germans responded that Jews were killed as Poles, Ukrainians, etc., the Israelis retorted that Jews were murdered as Jews, and sometimes by Poles and Ukrainians (Nieden 272–74). Such protests put the East German planners of Sachsenhausen in an awkward position. Given the Soviet and East German anti-Israeli policy, the inclusion of Israel in the Buchenwald Street of Nations, in the Sachsenhausen European Resistance museum, or on the Sachsenhausen obelisk was impossible. On the other hand, Albert Norden, a ranking Politburo member of Jewish descent who was intimately involved in the creation of the Sachsenhausen memorial, had initiated a campaign against Globke and West Germany, a campaign that received increased exposure in connection with the Eichmann trial. A Jewish exhibition, he realized, could be useful in that regard. Furthermore, the GDR was preparing to inaugurate its third concentration camp memorial, while the Federal Republic still had none (Dachau first opened in 1964). The East Germans did not want unwelcome publicity to overshadow a propaganda triumph it desperately needed: the country was losing citizens at a record pace, and just a few months after opening Sachsenhausen the East Germans would build the Berlin Wall. Norden expressed these concerns in a letter:

> Of course we cannot and may not even consider a "special Israeli exhibition." That is impossible by every political consideration. But the mass extermination of the Jews and what the antifascists did to protect the racially persecuted: this we must absolutely include in the Sachsenhausen exhibition. If we do not do that, then we supply material for those hostile smears that have already more than once

been voiced by world opinion: that the suffering of the Jews under
Hitler-fascism is not emphasized enough in the GDR.

(Cited in Nieden 274)

Just a few months before the Sachsenhausen memorial was sched-
uled to open, the East German government reconstructed, using
original materials, two Jewish barracks it had previously torn down,
and created a small Jewish exhibition. The post-1989 Brandenburg
historical commission criticized the exhibit as makeshift and dilettantish, full of platitudes and maintaining only tenuous links to the
actual situation in Sachsenhausen (Ministerium 236). There was no
information on the number of Jews in Sachsenhausen, the number
of Jewish deaths, or the special conditions of their captivity. The
fluid line — for Jews — between a concentration camp and an extermination camp was not thematized, and even the mass deportations of Jews to the killing centers was addressed only indirectly.

The exhibition contained pictures of the "hangmen" (Hitler,
Eichmann, and of course Globke) and their "taskmasters," the German industrialists. There were (undated) speeches by Ulbricht con-
demning the persecution of the Jews, and photographs with the
caption: "Thank you, Soviet soldiers!" The exhibition closed with
images intended to represent all the GDR had done for "its" Jews: a
constitution prohibiting discrimination based on race, creed, or nationality; the monument in the East Berlin Weißensee cemetery, the
largest remaining Jewish cemetery in Europe (through which the
government later planned to build a main traffic artery); a monument in the Großer Hamburger Straße in the formerly Jewish quar-
ter of Berlin; a Jewish geriatric home in Pankow; and a quote from
East German Rabbi Martin Riesenburger asserting that "in our state
the torch of anti-Semitism has gone out forever and religion is free."
These impressions were contrasted with the text: "The West German
state of imperialists and militarists is the boiling point for a new war
in Europe and hence the breeding ground for revanche and racial
persecution." That statement was followed by pictures of a West
German synagogue defaced by anti-Semitic graffiti, and a montage
of a West German neo-Nazi gathering. Under the text "Those behind the scenes then and now" the exhibition displayed pictures of
former Nazis who held leadership positions in the Bonn state, especially Globke. Adenauer himself was included in this category.

The remainder of the Sachsenhausen Jewish exhibition emphasized whatever Jewish resistance had occurred, and be it as far away

as Warsaw. Idealized sketches substituted for realia. Charles Hoffman writes:

> I was struck by the fact that the Jews in the sketches of camp life were almost all depicted in a heroic mode. They stood, in their striped inmate's uniforms, with heads held high and backs erect, as if they were waiting for the chance to strike out at their tormentors. The overwhelming sense of degradation and desperation that one sees in actual photos of concentration camp inmates was absent. This puzzled me until I heard a member of the Berlin Jewish community mention, in another context, that "the Germans can only see Jews as fighters against fascism. They can't see Jews as just plain Jews." This remark shed new light on the sketches at Sachsenhausen. Although the exhibit represented an admirable effort to (finally) acknowledge that the Jews were singled out as victims by the Nazis, it communicated the message that the Jews were persecuted because they were antifascists — not because they were Jews (184).

Hoffman correctly reads the message of the exhibit but he is wrong about the intentionality. The effort was neither belated nor admirable.

The Jewish exhibition emphasized Communist efforts to inspire, aid, and especially lead any resistance. A sketch (in the original directions for hanging the exhibit it is described as a "symbolic sketch about the fighting solidarity of the KPD with the persecuted Jews") shows, in condescending fashion, a strong, proletarian couple shielding a frightened Jewish doctor. (In a sense, it reflects the socialist realist sculpture, dominating the memorial site, of a Soviet soldier holding his cape protectively around inmates). The Communists, viewers learned, "educated" the Jews to antifascism, for "the Communists were the soul of the resistance."

The quintessential example of Communist assistance to the Jews is the story of Stefan Zerzy Zweig, who arrived in Buchenwald at the age of three and who was then hidden and protected by the underground Communist organization. Zweig features prominently in the heroic Fritz Cremer sculpture at the Buchenwald bell tower, and Bruno Apitz's novel *Nackt unter Wölfen* recounts the story in dramatic, indeed melodramatic form.[13] The novel was required reading in the GDR, but in the West its reception proved more reserved. The American literary scholar Ruth Angress (Ruth Klüger), herself a camp survivor, condemned the novel in harsh terms: "The Jew as victim of the Holocaust is literally infantilized, and put into the shadow by the Comrades, as if Jews had been only incidental victims compared to the genuine, ideological enemy who preserved his integrity and knew how to fight back" (216). The East German camp museums did seem able to acknowledge only those Jews who found what Ottomar Rothmann called the correct perspective. Even Stefan Zerzy Zweig appears to have disappointed in this regard. Responding to an inquiry about what eventually became of the famous Buchenwald child, the director of the camp museum wrote in 1977:

> He lived for many years in the GDR, where he had been educated and where he worked as a television cameraman. He occasionally made trouble, however, and the government approved his application to emigrate to Israel about seven or eight years ago. His father lived in Israel. Stefan first went to Vienna. Before he emigrated to Israel his father died, and Stefan stayed in Vienna. He also has contacts there to other Buchenwald comrades. We do not mention his current life unless special inquiries come, because he does not exactly represent the best example of a clear stand vis-à-vis our development. (Cited in Knigge 76–77)

Dead Jews (or people of Jewish descent) proved more useful for East German purposes. In the Buchenwald museum the emphasis was on Rudi Arndt, a young Communist of Jewish descent who was murdered in Buchenwald. Arndt figured prominently in SED mythology. He is one of two men of Jewish descent (the other is Herbert Baum) in Stephan Hermlin's book of resistance portraits *Die erste Reihe* (1951) (The Front Rank)[14] and he also looms large in the reports of five former Buchenwald inmates, *Buchenwald. Ein Konzentrationslager* (Buchenwald. A Concentration Camp) printed in 1986 in the GDR for a West German readership (Lagergemeinschaft 77–79). In *Kreuzweg Ravensbrück*, which contains portraits of 17 female "antifascist resistance fighters," the only woman of Jewish descent is Rosa Menzer, about whom we read that as a child she was raised in strict Jewish orthodoxy in Lithuania. But: "She had lost the belief in an amelioration of life through the 'coming of the Messiah' and now wanted to fight for it herself with the socialists whom she had meanwhile met. Freed from religious Judaism, Rosa . . . joins the Young Socialists . . . " (Jacobeit 127). Nonetheless, under the Nazis Menzer received an identity card with the "J" and is murdered in the camps, probably in March 1942. In Christa Wagner's *Geboren am See der Tränen* (Born on the Lake of Tears, 1987), an impressionistic collection of portraits dealing with Ravensbrück (a book her publisher, the Military Publishing House of the GDR, notes was intended as an emotionally moving book for young people [412]), the fact that Rosa Menzer was of Jewish heritage is not mentioned (53–54), and the reader is later surprised to discover that she is in Ravensbrück's Jewish barracks, which is being subjected to especially harsh persecution (78–81).

Silvia Nickel, a historian employed at the Sachsenhausen memorial site since 1984, has been working on the subject of Jews in Sachsenhausen. This subject was also the basis of her historical studies with Kurt Pätzold at the East Berlin Humboldt University. Nickel believes that around 1984 it became more acceptable to work on such themes in the GDR, in part because the government wanted to prepare for the Moses Mendelssohn anniversary in 1987 and the anniversary in 1988 of the so-called *Kristallnacht*. Nickel asserted that she never encountered any difficulties, either at university or at work, on account of her choice of theme, although she was subject to the restrictions applying to almost every East German historian: little access to certain archives and materials, and restricted access to Western scholarship. Furthermore, she was the first to work on the theme at Sachsenhausen, and had great difficulties gathering information, since the archives there had been "sieved." Only after 1989 was she able to travel to the West and to Israel.

Nickel recognized the neglect of the Holocaust in the East German exhibition, and had made efforts to remedy that. When I asked her why Jewish suffering had been downplayed in the pre-1989 exhibitions, she suggested three reasons. First, Sachsenhausen was not an extermination camp in the mode of Auschwitz, which was built expressly to deal with the "Final Solution." (That is also true of Buchenwald and Ravensbrück). Second, she thought that many Communists of Jewish descent who were prisoners in Sachsenhausen had little connection, either before or after the internment, with religious Judaism and did not consider themselves to be Jewish. These men set the tone for the exhibitions. Third, she acknowledged that the anti-Jewish persecutions of the 1950s, which forced many to choose between the Jewish community and the SED, must have affected the tone and the direction of the museum as well (Interview S.N.).

Harry Stein, the historian at Buchenwald, agreed that the anti-Jewish attacks of the 1950s, together with the official East German policy of anti-Zionism, clearly influenced the work at Buchenwald. Furthermore, former Buchenwald inmates such as Hermann Axen, a high ranking Party member of Jewish descent, decreed that Buchenwald had been a political camp, and that remained the Party line. The Jews were a politically heterogeneous group, and hence did not fit easily into the class-based categories of SED propaganda. Stein noted that little was "expressis verbis" forbidden — except research on the perpetrators — but the Party generated an atmosphere that led to self-censorship, which Stein admitted he himself had practiced. One did not work on Jews, he noted, "because one knew nobody would be interested and that one would not find a publisher" (Interview H.S.).

After 1989 Stein and other historians had little difficulty locating a publisher for a collection of documents dealing with Buchenwald's German Communist Kapos who had cemented the power of their organization by cooperating with the SS. The authors suggest that for non-German inmates, and especially for non-German, non-Communist inmates (i.e., the overwhelming majority during the war, since by 1944 German Communists constituted about 2% of the camp), there may not have appeared to be much of a difference between the terror of the German SS and that of the German KPD, which worked together with the SS. The authors note that available documentation does not demonstrate that the KPD shared Nazi racial anti-Semitism; indeed, the documentation appears to support Communist claims that they accepted Jews in their ranks, protected Jewish Communists in Buchenwald, and also protected numerous other non-Communist German or Western Jews. But the authors also point out that many Buchenwald Communists were German, and shared, often unconsciously, numerous stereotypes with the Nazis. Communists also employed such Nazi terms as "*Asoziale*" (asocial elements); like many of their contemporaries, they considered Gypsies to be scum, *Ostjuden* to be gangsters, and they viewed Slavic peoples with suspicion and condescension. In a situation where the Communists were often able to decide who would live and who would die, their prejudices could and did have deadly consequences.[15]

After 1989

After the opening of the Wall in 1989, the East German concentration camp memorials entered a period of crisis from which they have yet to emerge. The former directors of the Ravensbrück, Sachsenhausen, and Buchenwald memorials were dismissed and, after an extended period that included interim directors, replaced by western Germans with academic backgrounds in history. In the intervening periods, the remaining workers sometimes set about reorganizing the exhibitions themselves.

In Ravensbrück the old museum exhibition disappeared, and a large advertisement in English, French and German introduced the provisional exhibit. It emphasized the need for open-ended research and also for community involvement. The provisional exhibition was purposefully low key and centered around documentary material such as maps, diagrams, realia, and pictures. The commentary generally consisted of book or protocol excerpts from the inmates themselves. Several notebooks at one point in the exhibition explained new research directions the staff has undertaken, some with a pronounced gender-specific theme: medical experiments (forced sterilization, for example); the use of inmates in bordellos; the fate of pregnant women or of women with children. With the exception of Christa Wagner's book *Geboren am See der Tränen* of 1987, these aspects had been neglected in East Germany. The references to gender in Ravensbrück usually noted that the "woman's question" (analogously to the "Jewish question") had been solved in the GDR (as opposed to the West).[16]

The exhibition in the cell block at Ravensbrück has been retained due to its international character — many nations had erected memorials in former cells. The German historical commission responsible for Ravensbrück has, however, recommended that the exhibits by former socialist countries might be "carefully" reworked by those countries. The cell block museum has added exhibitions on the 20 July assassination attempt on Hitler, on the Jews in Ravensbrück, on Sinti and Roma, and on Christian resistance. The historical commission also recommended a new film, the addition of explanatory plaques to East German sculptures and monuments, and that the memorial site be expanded once the Soviet troops withdrew from the barracks they had created from the former camp. The tour of the camp is now slowly expanding to encompass the newly evacuated terrain.

The topography of Buchenwald is also changing. Günter Morsch, the new director of Sachsenhausen, once asserted that the East German government destroyed, either passively or actively, much of the original structure of the camps so that it might have fewer impediments for its own historical fantasies (*Die Wochenpost* 6 April 1993). To an extent, the Buchenwald memorial reflects that. In the original concept the bell tower was to be the center, and little of the original site was to be included, although that gradually changed over the years.[17] The reorganized memorial site is being expanded to include, for example, the "small camp," where numerous groups were quarantined, whence Jews were transported to Auschwitz, and where many inmates died. This site is currently overgrown; international youth groups are helping with the archeological work. Youth groups are also uncovering the ruins of buildings in which participants of the 20 July assassination plot were held, and the memorial site walking tour now includes topographies of the perpetrators, for example the ruins of SS houses and of the SS falconry. The memorial site has added outdoor memorials to Sinti and Roma, and to Jewish victims. Stein noted that Jewish organizations had lobbied for such a memorial for decades (26).

Buchenwald's "second history" as a Soviet internment camp from 1945–1950 poses special challenges for a historical museum. A government historical commission recommended a new exhibition building be built outside the confines of the current camp, behind the former storehouse that now contains the museum documenting the Nazi camp. The spatial distance would help avoid a crude equation of the two camps, and would also be located in the vicinity of the mass graves made public after 1989. This building was begun in 1995. The graves, over which in the past forty years a young forest has grown up, are now tended as a cemetery. The grave sites have been marked as well as possible; exhumations will be avoided. In a small clearing relatives and friends have erected simple crosses or stones commemorating those in the graves. Intended or not, the ad hoc memorials stand in marked contrast to the bombastically heroicized monuments of East German origin. It has become a site of dialogue; in 1995 a hand-lettered ribbon read:

> In remembrance of my poor, beloved grandfather on the fiftieth anniversary of his death. He was a retired general and victim of his soldierly obedience to authority, which made no exception for Hitler. I wish he had refused. May he rest in peace.

The staff of the would-be museum stands before a formidable task, given the lack of documents and realia. Oral histories and other materials are being gathered, and the opening of former Soviet archives in Russia and elsewhere is providing additional information.

A third stage in the coming to terms with the history of Buchenwald is the role of the camp as a memorial site in the GDR. The historical commission recommended an exhibit on this theme at the bell tower. The third stage, however, remains subordinate to the museal work relating to Nazi and Soviet uses of the camp.

At Sachsenhausen the East German buildings and monuments will also remain (with the possible exception of a leaking roof over the ruins of the gas chamber), including the obelisk celebrating political opposition. As in Buchenwald, the camp museum exhibition is being replaced with a more scholarly presentation.

The Sachsenhausen Museum for the Antifascist Resistance Struggle of the European Peoples has been dismantled, although some stone monuments that are part of a wall remain, as do the stained glass murals depicting defiant inmates and a red flag. Since the collapse of East Germany the museum has featured several exhibitions on Jews, including one on Jews in Sachsenhausen and one displaying an encyclopedia of enmity against the Jews. The entry on anti-Zionism critically examined the East German use of the term. According to one of the employees at the memorial, some Communists felt that the former underemphasis on Jewish victims was now being countervailed by an overemphasis.

The mass graves outside Sachsenhausen demand a memorial as well, and the historical commission has made recommendations similar to those for Buchenwald. In 1993 the graves were marked by large wooden crosses, but they lay outside the camp on ground used as a military base. After the withdrawal of the Soviet and East German troops, formal cemeteries were erected.

Since 1989 the memorial sites have over and again confronted the question of whose history should be commemorated, and in what fashion. When the Buchenwald museum conducted a symposium based on E.M. Remarque's *Der Funke Leben* (The Spark of Life, 1952), a novel set in a camp clearly based on Buchenwald, the keynote speaker Wilfried Schoeller, a western German literary critic with intimate knowledge of the former GDR, took the occasion to criticize what he called "history with blinders" in the former East German discourse on Buchenwald. His major example was the East German classic *Nackt unter Wölfen*. Schoeller's audience, many of whom were former Communist prisoners in the camp, reacted angrily with catcalls and hisses. Several people indignantly left the room.

In 1991 the city of Fürstenberg began implementing its plans for the commercial development of land that was technically part of the Ravensbrück concentration camp, though outside the current memorial. Next to the Street of Nations, a cobblestone road that had been built by Ravensbrück inmates, a supermarket was built. Angry international protests from former inmates stopped construction and left the building empty, but the incident underscored the tensions between communities and the memorial sites. The reasons were manifold. Those in favor of the supermarket pointed to the desperate economic situation in the East and the need for jobs. (There was little eastern German protest against the supermarket). They could also point out that many other communities in both East and West Germany used former concentration camp buildings or land for commercial or government purposes. (It was not mentioned in most press releases on the controversy that the Soviets used the Ravensbrück site as a military garrison). Others associated the memorial site not so much with the Nazis as with the East German dictatorship's instrumentalization of the Nazi past. Yet others resented the association of their city with a concentration camp, a phenomenon one often encountered/encounters in the former West Germany as well (Dachau, for instance). In the East, communities for the first time had the right to protest *against* a memorial site (Koonz, "Germany's" 92).

The historical commission concluded that the Street of Nations was inappropriate for commercial buildings or advertising, and suggested the supermarket parking lot be used as the main parking lot for the camp museum. The building itself should be used for traveling exhibitions. The commission also suggested that the building be shared by the city, which could use it as a library, archive, or cultural center. With this compromise, the commission hoped that the city would become less antagonistic toward the site. But in 1998 the building remained empty.

The collapse of the police state has brought more ominous forms of protest as well: since 1989 there have been arson attacks on Ravensbrück and Sachsenhausen. The attack on Sachsenhausen was directed at the Jewish exhibition and destroyed most of it. By 1996 a provisional exhibition on Jews had been erected, and a new Jewish museum, the design of which is based on the results of an international competition, opened in November 1997.

A final problem — a massive one — is how to incorporate into redesigned memorial sites the Soviet use of Sachsenhausen and Buchenwald from 1945–1950 as internment centers. If many eastern Germans have ambivalent feelings about the East German anti-fascist memorials, feelings that can lead in some cases to a desire for repression and "normalcy," the interest in the Soviet uses of the camps is keen. In part the interest results from the enforced taboo surrounding this subject in the GDR. The suffering and death of those Germans interned by the Soviets assumes a synecdochical relationship for many to their own suffering under the East German dictatorship.

As I have noted, the historical commissions have suggested separate museums and are careful to insist on exhibits that compare and differentiate, hence avoiding a facile equation of brown and red dictatorships. But Andreas Nachama, representing the Central Committee of Jews in Germany, rejected the Brandenburg commission's recommendations in the strongest terms. He believed the commission was equating the crimes of Hitler with those of Stalin, and he resented plans to commemorate "victims and perpetrators" together. After 1945, he argued, no one — except those who had been persecuted by and freed from Nazi tyranny — was innocent (Ministerium 191). Rosel Vadehra-Jonas of the Organization of the Persecuted of Nazism agreed (Ministerium 192). On the other hand, the Chairperson for the Association of Victims of Stalinist Persecution in Germany could not understand such resistance; in his opinion, the commission's recommendations do not go far enough (Ministerium 172–74).

Negotiating these minefields will be no easy task for the newly reformed staffs at the memorial sites, and political pressure of a new kind, hinted one staff member to me, is also pronounced. Especially Sachsenhausen, on the light rail line to the newly unified capital of Germany, is destined to become *the* concentration camp museum in Germany, and how the new exhibition takes shape is of intense interest not only to the former inmates, but also to politicians of various colors. In Sachsenhausen the new Germany will define itself to the world. Initiated by Chancellor Helmut Kohl, two recent German projects of remembering — the Museum of the Federal Republic in Bonn, and the central memorial site of the Federal Republic, Schinkel's newly redesigned *Neue Wache* in Berlin — give an indication of the possible parameters. The history museum in Bonn is brutally frank about the Holocaust but only briefly mentions Globke in Adenauer's postwar government. The *Neue Wache* reflects newer Holocaust historiography in that it specifically mentions groups that have been too often forgotten in one or the other Germany, or in both: Jews, homosexuals, Sinti and Roma. But in the same breath it mentions the Germans victimized by tyranny (*Gewaltherrschaft*), thus blurring distinctions between German victims and victims of Germans.[18] It does not specify what has become of the remains of the Unknown Antifascist Resistance Fighter buried there by the East Germans to express their religious/nationalist imaginings.

Discussing the ongoing debates about the proper memorial for the Berlin "Topography of Terror," the archeological remains of the former Gestapo headquarters, James Young mused that perhaps the most fitting Holocaust memorial is one that is unfinished. There is much to recommend this view: as process, an unfinished memorial resists the monumentalization and stasis so often attending to markers that, over time, can turn into meaningless ciphers. An unfinished memorial remains flexible, open to discussion and revision, open to the filigrees of memory. Such sites resist the "polished, finished veneer of a death mask." In a sense, that describes the state of eastern German memorials to National Socialism today.

Notes

[1]   David Bathrick also describes such emplotments in the introduction to his study *The Power of Words*.

[2]   These numbers are unreliable and probably inflated.

[3]   In this chapter I pay rather more attention to Buchenwald and Sachsenhausen, both of which I visited regularly before 1989. Ravensbrück I first visited after 1989.

[4]   At the Sachsenhausen memorial site there was a Museum of the Antifascist Resistance Struggle of the European Peoples, which dealt with fascism on an international scale, a *Lager*-Museum (I call it the camp museum), which dealt more specifically with the situation in Sachsenhausen, and the Jewish museum, located in a reconstructed barracks.

[5]   The inmates are well-fed and well-dressed and not immediately recognizable as former prisoners. They should instead symbolize freed antifascist resistance fighters who embody the East German heritage. The shape of these sculptures was the subject of considerable discussion (S. Becker 285–86).

[6]   Niethammer's recent collection of documents about the behavior of German Communist Kapos at Buchenwald reveals that the trope of solidarity constructed with these exhibits was far more problematic in the reality. In their cooperation with the Nazis, the German Communists at Buchenwald were sometimes in part responsible for the murder of Soviet soldiers. This was a damning charge against many of them in the postwar East German purges, but it did not prevent the Moscow faction of the SED from stylizing Buchenwald as an anvil of German-Soviet cooperation.

[7]   See for example the films *Befreier und Befreite* (Liberator and Liberated, 1992) by Helke Sander or *Verschleppt ans Ende der Welt* (Dragged to the End of the World, 1993) by Freya Klier.

[8]   Current research suggests that altogether, the Soviets interned approximately 240,000 people, of whom between 78,000 and 95,643 died. (Herf, *Divided* 73).

[9]   Young, *Texture* 77. Young's "reading" of Buchenwald is in its essence correct, but his text contains several errors. The Reichstag was not in East Germany, as he implies (*Texture* 72); Jews were indeed accorded special rights as Jews and not merely as antifascists (73); Buchenwald was not the only truly national East German memorial to the Nazi period — Sachsenhausen and perhaps Ravensbrück also fit that description (73). Buchen-

wald was not the seedbed of the German Communist party (73); Goethe is not usually described as a philosopher (74); the Americans did not occupy Thüringen for three years (75); "Vereinigung" (75) and "Thälmann" (78) are misspelled; *Neues Deutschland* newspaper is not run by the Social Democrats (79).

[10] The title, like much in the camps, utilizes Christian symbolism to refer to the martyrdom of Communists.

[11] See Herbert, *Fremdarbeiter*. In August 1944 the German Reich had 7,615,970 foreign workers registered: 1.9 million POWs and 5.7 million civilians. This does not include concentration camp prisoners. Herbert asserts that this subject has been ignored by West German historians (11).

[12] The memorial stone was erected in 1954, but the Hebrew inscription was first added in 1988 as part of the country-wide commemoration of the 1938 pogrom.

[13] For more on this novel, see chapter 4.

[14] For more on this book, see chapter 4.

[15] Niethammer 51–52. See also Semprun 257 ff.

[16] There has been little work done on the gender-specific aspects of the East German memorials. Claudia Koonz comments that the sculptures at Buchenwald and Sachsenhausen feature defiant men with raised fists, while the statues of women at Ravensbrück show them as generally passive. ("Between" 267).

[17] Röll 25. See also Knigge 71–72.

[18] Saul Friedländer's response to Andreas Hillgruber can stand as a comment on the *Neue Wache* memorial as well: "There are two opposite categories of victims, whereby part of the erstwhile bystanders becomes the new category of victims. [Such logic], long a basic staple of an image of the past carried by part of the West German population, essentially that of the contemporaries of the Third Reich, thus became an element of the learned discourse. This move from the periphery to the center of the public scene is of no small significance" (33–34).

Ravensbrück.
A Soviet tank at the entrance to the memorial site.
(All photographs by the author unless otherwise noted.)

Ruins of the gas chamber at Sachsenhausen.
The plaque remembers Soviet POWs murdered there,
and only them.

*The forty-meter obelisk at Sachsenhausen. It features only
red triangles, the badge of the political prisoner. At the base
is a Soviet soldier holding his cape protectively around two
former inmates, the symbolic leaders of East Germany.
Courtesy of Fotothek, Gedenkstätte Sachsenhausen.*

Sachsenhausen.
A Soviet soldier protecting two former inmates.

One of many monuments commemorating the death marches.
The badge in the upper left as well as the one worn by the
first prisoner is that of the political prisoner.

Sachsenhausen Camp Museum.
An idealized sketch celebrating the Communists as
"The true leaders of Germany."

*"The Liberated Prisoners" in front of the bell tower at the
Buchenwald memorial site. At the left is Stefan Zerzy Zweig,
here transformed into an older child and resistance fighter.
Courtesy of Archiv, Gedenkstätte Buchenwald*

Two representations of female prisoners at Ravensbrück.
Statues of women at Ravensbrück generally depict more passive
suffering than the defiant portrayals of male prisoners at
Buchenwald and Sachsenhausen. Courtesy of Gedenkstätte
Ravensbrück. Photo by Anneliese Bonitz.

A memorial stone in Buchenwald:
"Between November 1938 and February 1939 approximately
10,000 Jews — boys, men, old men — were imprisoned here.
600 of them were murdered in bestial fashion during this time.
They died as victims of fascist racial insanity."
The stone was set in 1954; the Hebrew was added in 1988.
Courtesy of Archiv, Gedenkstätte Buchenwald.

Sachsenhausen.
The obelisk celebrating Communist martyrdom as seen from the
site of a mass grave resulting from Soviet use of the camp.

3: In the Melting Pot of Socialism: East German Jews

> *I am neither a Jew nor a Zionist,*
> *though, certainly, it would be no*
> *crime to be either.*
> Paul Merker, 1955

> *The Nazis wiped out the Jewish*
> *people — but the Stalinists pre-*
> *ferred to liquidate everything*
> *that was Jewish in the Jews.*
> Wolf Biermann, 1994

In one of its inaugural acts, the first democratically elected East German *Volkskammer* (parliament) issued a statement in 1990 accepting responsibility for the legacy of National Socialism and apologizing to the Jews. The new government thus broke decisively with the policies of the Socialist Unity Party, which had severed itself from the fascist past and, not incidentally, from the duty of indemnification. While the media rightly accorded this part of the *Volkskammer* statement much attention, a second aspect remained generally unnoticed. The East German parliament expressed regret for "the persecution and denigration of Jewish citizens in our country also after 1945" (*Allgemeine Jüdische Wochenzeitung* 19 April 1990).

The second apology surprised casual observers, for the SED had supported the minuscule Jewish congregations with considerable subsidies, rebuilding synagogues and caring for Jewish cemeteries. As official "victims of fascism" East German Jews had received higher pensions and could retire earlier; they also had enjoyed advantageous medical treatment as well as housing and educational privileges. During the extensive 1988 commemorations of the 1938 pogrom, the East German government had underscored its preferential treatment of East German Jews.

Additionally, Jews or people of Jewish heritage had played an important role building the German Democratic Republic. In the 1950s numerous theater directors were of Jewish descent, as was the most famous East German actress, Helene Weigel. Prominent writers as diverse as Wolf Biermann, Thomas Brasch, Stephan Hermlin,

Stefan Heym, Günter Kunert, Anna Seghers, and Arnold Zweig came or come from Jewish backgrounds. Many of the first diplomats and politicians representing the GDR were of Jewish descent, and not a few of them attained high government positions — one thinks of Alexander Abusch, Albert Norden, or Hermann Axen. Gregor Gysi, the leader of the SED successor party PDS (*Partei des Demokratischen Sozialismus*, or Party of Democratic Socialism), is of Jewish heritage, and his father Klaus Gysi functioned in leading political positions. Eastern German historian Olaf Groehler asserts that never before in history had Jews had so much influence in German politics, art, and scholarship as in the Soviet Occupation Zone and later GDR (GSA 1).

In light of this, one understands the assertion by Peter Honigmann, an East German Jewish intellectual, that Jews lived more securely in his country than anywhere else (105). Honigmann's opinion was and is by no means an isolated one, and one could wonder for what the *Volkskammer* had to apologize. Yet despite the government privileges accorded them, Jews belonging to the Jewish Communities in the GDR numbered only about 350 in the late 1980s, and the western German scholar Lothar Mertens predicted that within the foreseeable future there might have been no more practicing Jews in East Germany ("Schwindende"). One need only compare that situation with West Germany, where the relative as well as absolute number of religious Jews was far greater.

Despite its gestures of support for the Jewish Communities, the SED established systemic limits to the preoccupation with Judaism, so that, at least until the mid 1980s, one could concern oneself with the subject under the condition that one treat it as a matter of historical interest only (P. Honigmann 105, 111). Furthermore, the secular, Marxist state subjected all religious denominations to measures designed to help them wither away. Finally, the Stalinist anti-Zionist campaign of the 1950s devastated the Jewish Communities and contributed decisively to the desolate demographic situation of East German Jews in the later 1980s. If, as shown in the *Volkskammer* declaration, the GDR had experienced difficulty coming to terms with the fascist past, it had encountered yet more difficulty addressing its own Stalinist past. Both lapses affected the Jews.

National Socialists persecuted Jews and Communists, though for different reasons; nonetheless, the SED often coupled the two groups, thus rendering it difficult, as Irene Runge has pointed out, to develop a Jewish identity apart from SED ideology (Cited in Noll 770). Within the equation of Jewish-Communist togetherness, however, differences existed. For a brief time after the war, the Communists rejected Jewish material claims altogether (Groehler, "Juden" 53–54). Jews constituted *Opfer des Faschismus* (Victims of Fascism), while Communists maintained the title *Kämpfer gegen den Faschismus* (Fighters against Fascism). That accorded with the SED view of Jews as "passive" victims, and the terminology carried practical consequences. Pensions of the *Opfer* (Victims), for example, were higher than those of the average citizen, but less than those of the *Kämpfer* (Fighters). Eastern German historian Helmut Eschwege has recorded examples of Jewish resistance fighters who were not awarded the status of *Kämpfer*. Eschwege has also discussed attempts of Jews during the 1950s to regain property that had been expropriated by the Nazis. They learned that as "passive," non-political victims they did not qualify as "antifascists" and were hence ineligible for individual restitution payments. The expropriated property became state property or was awarded to non-Jewish citizens, whereupon many Jews left the Democratic Republic for the Federal Republic, which maintained a more generous reparation policy.[1] The subsequent material support given to the East German Jewish Communities by the state never compensated for the wealth the Communities had lost to the state. In 1991, soon after German reunification, the Council of Jews in Germany filed claims to 1270 properties that had formerly been "Aryanized" and then socialized. (Ostow, "Imperialist" 239).

Several purges in the 1950s also affected East German Jews and especially the Jewish Communities. The controversy surrounding public figures with any connection to the alleged American spy Noel Field, combined with the Soviet campaign against "rootless cosmopolitanism," led to an initial purge in 1950. The government suspended Paul Merker, State Secretary in the Ministry of Agriculture and a member of the Politburo, from the Party and from his posts; while in Mexican exile during the 1940s, Merker, who was not Jewish, had called for creation of a Jewish state and for reparations to Jews living in Germany and abroad. To be sure, the Party also purged other non-Jews at this time, and some prominent Jews or people of Jewish descent, for example the famous writer and President of the East German Writers' Association Anna Seghers, remained apparently inviolate. Many of those affected had spent the

Second World War in Western exile, which in the ensuing Cold War atmosphere often served as an accusation in itself. But recently available SED documents demonstrate that as early as March 1949 citizens of Jewish descent were singled out by government security for special attention on account of their Jewishness (Kessler 152). Autobiographies of personalities as diverse as Heinz Brandt, Carl Jakob Danzinger, and Helmut Eschwege, all former East German Communists, demonstrate that their Jewish background was seen as a disadvantage (Kessler 157).

These actions occurred within the context of an anti-Semitic campaign in the Soviet Union, one which extended to the Soviet occupation army in the GDR, where Soviet officers of Jewish descent were also purged (Thompson 78, 82). Jürgen Kuczynski, who by his own admission "suddenly and rather brutally" lost his position as head of the Society for German-Soviet Friendship, and who could not thereafter join the Central Committee of the SED, blames Soviet anti-Semitism for his fall, although he remains careful to spare his Party. In his autobiographical *Dialog mit meinem Urenkel* (Dialogue with My Great-Grandchild, 1983), he writes curtly: "You surely know that at times during Stalin's rule anti-Semitic attitudes occasionally developed in the Soviet Union. By the way, these attitudes were never taken over by our Party leadership, not even in the smallest way (51–52, my trans.). East German author Bodo Uhse's article launching the East German attack on "stateless, rootless cosmopolites, the bearded and hook-nosed enemies of national sovereignty, the international destroyers of a true people's culture" appears to contradict Kuczynski's assertion.[2]

The general situation of East bloc Jews worsened perceptibly in late 1951. In September Rudolf Slánský, a man of Jewish descent, lost his position as Secretary General of the Czech Communist Party, and a month later he was imprisoned. In November 1952 the state charged Slánský and thirteen other former Party officials with crimes including Zionism; in a show trial the prosecution as well as the East bloc press emphasized the Jewishness of eleven defendants. In December 1952 the Czech government hanged eleven of the accused, including Slánský, while three received life sentences.

On 13 January 1953 the Soviet government announced it had uncovered a "doctors' plot" designed to assassinate Soviet leaders. The government arrested nine doctors, seven of Jewish origin. Soviet press releases spoke of "terrorist Jewish doctors," who were connected with the American Jewish Joint Distribution Committee and hence allegedly with American intelligence.[3] Two doctors died in prison; the Soviets freed and exonerated the others after Stalin's death in March 1953.

These events had direct ramifications for East German Jews. In December 1952, after the execution of Slánský, the SED circulated a pamphlet outlining the "lessons" of the Slánský trial and warning against Zionism or such organizations as Joint. The document, which was later withdrawn from circulation and was not available even to those with a permit allowing use of "special research literature" (Kessler 154), employs near-Nazi rhetoric (Kessler 154); indeed, one need only substitute "Jewish-Bolshevik" for "Zionist-Capitalist" to underscore the similarities. At the same time the document draws on the tradition of the *Protocols of the Elders of Zion* to support its argument for the connection of Judaism with capitalism. Jeffrey Herf correctly notes that this denunciation, written by the high-ranking East German Party ideologue Hermann Matern, "rested on an old anti-Semitic stereotype," and that it "presented the good old international Jewish conspiracy, this time in a Communist discourse" ("East German" 17). Olaf Groehler's archival research leads him to characterize Matern as a Communist who most probably was infected with Stalinist anti-Semitism ("Umgang" 236).

In further actions, the East German government obtained from the Organization of the Persecuted of Nazism lists of Jewish Community leaders and also names of East German Jews who had, until 1950, received packages from Joint (Thompson 125). The government searched offices of the Jewish Communities, seizing papers and books. Leo Zuckermann, the former head of President Wilhelm Pieck's chancellery, was one of the most prominent officials of Jewish descent affected by these events; in early January he took sanctuary in West Berlin.[4]

On 13 January, the day the Soviet government announced the so-called doctors' plot, Julius Meyer, Head of the East German Jewish *Länder* (States') Association and a former *Volkskammer* member, fled to West Berlin, together with the leaders of the Leipzig, Erfurt, and Dresden communities.[5] On the 14th the leaders of the Halle and Schwerin communities also left for the West, followed soon thereafter by those of Eisenach and Magdeburg. On the 18th, police throughout the GDR searched numerous offices and houses belonging to Jews (Thompson 135). According to Thompson, one

hundred Jews or people of Jewish descent were dismissed from positions in the Foreign Office, and some were arrested (139). The Berlin Jewish Community split between East and West. The turmoil
continued into July 1953 — after Stalin's death — and even such
high-ranking Party officials as Albert Norden and Hermann Axen
lost favor, although they had vocally and energetically supported the
SED position regarding anti-Zionism, anti-restitution, and anti-
Americanism. As Robin Ostow points out, "The GDR government
publicly constructed Jews as personifications of the external and internal threats to national stability" ("Imperialist" 231).

East German government officials maintained that they directed
their policies against "Zionism," not against Jews, but among those
purged in the 1950s were people who considered themselves to be
neither Zionists nor, indeed, Jews. Jürgen Kuczynski's argument —
that the purges were anti-Semitic but directed from the Soviet Union — also lacks plausibility, at least if applied to "anti-Zionist"
purges in the GDR occurring after Stalin's death, at a time when the
Soviets were rehabilitating those accused of participating in the
"doctors' plot." More likely, Ulbricht employed anti-Zionism as a
code word that enabled him to utilize (some) Jews as scapegoats; as
late as 1968 the GDR justified its invasion of Czechoslovakia by asserting that Zionist elements had assumed control of the government (Korey 151), and at that time thousands of Jews left Poland
because of a government anti-Zionist campaign.

Even during the worst period of the 1950s, however, some East
German public figures of Jewish descent — notably such cultural
icons as Arnold Zweig, Anna Seghers, or Helene Weigel — remained relatively inviolate. Indeed, as Paul O'Doherty points out, in
the late 1950s the three most important East German cultural functionaries — Writers' Union President (1952–1977) Anna Seghers,
Honorary President of the Academy of Arts (1953–1968) Arnold
Zweig, and Minister of Culture (1958–1961) Alexander Abusch —
were of Jewish origin ("German-Jewish" 273). And although Jews
were fleeing Stalinist persecution in the GDR, five of the twelve
people contributing eulogies to Stalin in the East German magazine
Sinn und Form were of Jewish background: Abusch, Hermlin,
Seghers, the playwright Friedrich Wolf, and Zweig ("Zum Tode").
In the 1950s the SED funded the restoration of a synagogue in Erfurt and one in Berlin. A Jewish-run geriatric home as well as an or-
phanage, both in Pankow, continued to operate.[6] Stephan Hermlin

and others have often argued that despite the injustices of the period, the situation of Jews in the GDR never grew as dire as in other East bloc countries.[7] German history forced East Germany to accede to the Soviet Union, but it also sensitized the SED to accusations of anti-Semitism.

Nonetheless, Herf's recent investigations into the case of Paul Merker make clear that Merker was persecuted due to his insistence on placing the "Jewish Question" at the center of East German discourse, not on the periphery. The SED planned to make Merker the German Slánský; out of various political considerations he was instead tried in secret in March 1955, after having been in prison since December 1952. At the trial he was sentenced to an additional eight years (the same court later freed him when the political winds shifted). Along with the denunciation from 1952, Herf considers the court verdict, now available to historians, important evidence of East German anti-Semitism ("East German" 22). Merker also reported being subjected to anti-Semitic taunts and slurs in prison ("East German" 21), an allegation made by others arrested during that time as well (Kessler 157). In response to charges brought against him in 1952 and 1955, Merker wrote a 38-page defense in 1956 that includes the assertion: "I am neither a Jew nor a Zionist, though, certainly, it would be no crime to be either" (cited by Herf, "East German" 23). But, as Herf notes: "As of December 1952-January 1953, it was clear that the silence concerning the Jewish Question in East Germany was no longer primarily a result of the inadequacies of Marxist-Leninist theories of fascism and antifascism. By then, East German Communists, Jews and non-Jews, understood that sympathy for the Jews as expressed by Merker was not only 'incorrect'; it was dangerous" ("East German" 19). The persecution of Merker, it should be noted, continued well after Stalin's death, and Merker, who died in 1969, was never fully rehabilitated politically by the SED. Alexander Abusch, who is cited by O'Doherty as an example of East German tolerance toward Jews, was able to "rehabilitate" himself by testifying that he had absolutely no interest in Jewish affairs, by denouncing Merker (Herf, "East German" 18–19), and by agreeing to work as an informant for the secret police.[8] Anna Seghers's husband also testified against Merker. Eastern German journalist and essayist Christoph Dieckmann suspects that Stephan Hermlin, of Jewish descent, may also have been pressured by his government into allowing himself to be turned into a larger-than-life antifascist hero with a falsified biography.[9]

The effects of the East bloc anti-Zionist campaign, the Slánský trial, and the "doctors' plot" devastated the Jewish Communities in the GDR. According to Thompson, between 1945 and 1953 half the practicing Jews remaining in that country left for the West (287). The leaders of most Jewish Communities fled in 1953; the government replaced them with dependable SED members who insured that the Communities would become (unlike the Protestant church), politically as well as religiously orthodox. Robin Ostow summarizes the effects of the purges:

> The anti-Jewish terror of the early 1950s served three major purposes. First it destroyed the GDR Jewish Communities as grass roots organizations with their own political basis. . . . Second, it effected an almost complete separation of its Jews and its Jewish Communities from Western organizations and influences. And third, as the Nazi Aryanization of businesses and professions twenty years previously had demonstrated, the removal of an entire social group from desirable positions — or from society as a whole — creates new opportunities and the resulting alleviation of some political frustrations for the rest of the population.[10]

Ostow elsewhere claims that for "most of the four decades of the German Democratic Republic, Jewish life barely existed, even for the Jews themselves" ("Imperialist" 228). East Germany maintained the Jewish Communities as what Thompson terms "museum pieces," useful totems that demonstrated freedom of religion in the GDR, or that illustrated the preferential treatment accorded victims of fascism. SED Jewish leaders, for example Helmut Aris, regularly condemned "resurgent" anti-Semitism in the Federal Republic, or attacked that country's reparations policy, or congratulated the SED on its successful effort to eliminate anti-Semitism in East Germany.[11] In the 1980s they assisted East German efforts to attain Most Favored Nation trading status with the United States. Otherwise, the tiny Jewish Communities exercised little influence in the GDR.

Various government restrictions helped insure the marginalized status of the East German Jewish Communities. A newsletter published by the Organization of East German Jewish Communities was not available through a mail subscription, and the state monitored its contents closely. Invitations to artistic events with a pronounced "Jewish" theme were restricted, and the SED prohibited advertise-

ments with placards or in the media. The state-controlled press reported little about the Communities and their activities (Maser 161–
62). Western German author Peter Maser commented sardonically
that East German Jews must have had the impression that their government honored dead Jews at every opportunity (the 1988 "*Ge-
denkepidemie*" or "commemoration epidemic" provided an example
of this), but demonstrated little interest in a dialogue with living
ones (162).

Biased East German journalistic coverage of Israel proved a recurring source of tension between Jews and the state. Again, SED ideology claimed to differentiate between anti-Zionism and anti-
Semitism, but a cartoon lampooning American imperialism could
feature the imperialist with a crooked, "Jewish" nose (P. Honigmann 101). In 1968 Simon Wiesenthal decried the similarities between the East German press and Nazi propaganda, asserting that
thirty-nine people who had maintained influential media posts during National Socialism occupied similar ones in the GDR (Korey
151).

In the later 1970s Peter Dittmar documented manipulative East
German press reporting on Israel, a feature which continued into the
1980s.[12] Peter Kirchner, the Chairperson of the East Berlin Jewish
Community, commented in November 1982:

> Because the official political line of the state is anti-Israeli and pro-
> Arab, the mass media especially emphasize the anti-Israeli compo-
> nent. They put it so much in the foreground that we can no longer
> avoid seeing the nearly identical relationship of this anti-Israeli at-
> titude to traditional anti-Judaism. If an adolescent is confronted
> almost daily — due to political reasons — with negative data about
> the Israeli Jews, he or she can hardly avoid transferring these nega-
> tive depictions to the Jews in his or her environment.
>
>   (Cited in Mertens, "Schwindende" 143)

In the later 1980s Peter Honigmann asserted: "As a rule, the news-
papers depict only the shadow side of Israeli life, and they do that
almost every day." He added that the majority of East German Jews
perceived that as "very burdensome" (113). The American rabbi
Isaac Neuman, who during 1988 served briefly in East Berlin, after-
wards spoke of a "demonization" of Israel in the East German
press,[13] and also in 1988 the President of the East German Organization of Jewish Communities, Siegmund Rotstein, asserted in a
West German interview that a causal relation existed between anti-

Semitic occurrences in the GDR and the East German media coverage of Israel (*Süddeutsche Zeitung* 15/16 Oct. 1988).

In 1984 Peter Kirchner had characterized Israeli-GDR relations as a taboo subject (Ostow, *Jews* 20), but during the turbulent days of November 1989 the Organization of East German Jewish Communities declared its "elemental interest" in the fate of Israel, whose right of existence, the statement insisted, could not be placed into question. The Organization demanded that the government establish diplomatic relations with Israel and take steps to normalize relations between the two countries (*Neues Deutschland* 6 Nov. 1989). The 1990 *Volkskammer* declaration then apologized for the former "hypocrisy and hostility of the official East German political policy towards Israel." Those policies had included armaments shipments to Arab states and to the PLO.

Such changes were dramatic, but even before November 1989 significant improvements in East German Jewish life had occurred. In January 1986 the GDR sent a delegation to the (Zionist) World Jewish Congress in Jerusalem, a gesture Lothar Mertens characterized as "sensational," ("Schwindende" 143), though it was not covered in the East German media (Mertens, "Staatlich" 147). In May 1986 Irene Runge, who had accompanied the delegation to Israel, began to organize contacts between the Berlin Jewish Communities and other Berliners of Jewish descent. Beginning in September 1987 groups calling themselves *Wir für uns* (We for Us) or *Die Neuen* (The New Ones) met regularly once or twice monthly, and they organized a children's group as well. Few of these people ultimately joined the Community, and the more religiously orthodox Community members often viewed them with suspicion, but these "outsiders" constituted a context and a support structure for the Community (Maser 164–65, Ammer 22–23). At times up to 200 people would attend the group meetings, although after November 1989 these numbers declined dramatically (Mertens, "Der politische" 124). After the end of the GDR Kirchner and others have suggested that some of those newcomers were following the dictates of the Party, which was interested, for state reasons, in preserving East German Jews from extinction and also in continuing to exercise influence and control (Kirchner "Die jüdische" 35–36; Burgauer 209).

In 1988 the GDR commemorated the fiftieth anniversary of the November pogrom with considerable éclat. A DEFA documentary film on the history of Berlin's Jews opened festively in January.

Throughout the country committees and organizations unveiled plaques commemorating Jewish victims of National Socialism. Memorial ceremonies took place at the Humboldt University, the Academy of Arts, The Academy of Sciences, and many other institutions. On 8 November the government convened a special session of the *Volkskammer*, during which *Volkskammer* President Horst Sindermann and Siegmund Rotstein held memorial speeches in the presence of Party Chief Erich Honecker. The program appeared in German and Hebrew.

Also in 1988 Honecker met several times with Heinz Galinski, the leader of the West German and West Berlin Jewish Communities; among other things, they agreed to establish a *Centrum Judaicum* in the former synagogue in the Oranienburger Straße of East Berlin. In 1988 Edgar Miles Bronfman, President of the Jewish World Congress, visited the GDR, as did Gerhart Riegner, the honorary president of that Congress.

The abundant attention accorded East German Jews in 1988 undoubtedly improved their situation, though Western observers often viewed the SED campaign with skepticism. Especially West Germans argued that the SED intended to distract attention from its growing difficulties with a restive Protestant church that provided a haven for dissidents; that it wished to parade its antifascism while implicitly or explicitly attacking the Federal Republic; and that it hoped to win the support of the North American Jewish lobby for a visit of Erich Honecker to the United States and for the classification of the GDR as a Most Favored Nation trading partner (for instance, *Frankfurter Allgemeine Zeitung* 19 Nov. 1988). In fact, Bronfman announced his support for these latter two measures during a press conference in East Berlin (*Neues Deutschland* 19 Oct. 1988).

The commemorations of 1988 addressed the pre-1945 history of German Jews, but they avoided the brisant theme of Jewish history in the Soviet Occupied Zone or in the GDR. Erich Honecker expressed the Party line on 8 November:

> Our country became a home for all those fellow Jewish citizens who survived the fascist inferno or who returned from emigration. Many of them served as activists in the building of a new society. Respected, appreciated, and honored, they made lasting contributions to our socialist fatherland. (Cited in Maser 159)

Honecker voiced an expurgated version of history, of course, but it was one to which more critical thinkers often adhered, if with variations. The writer Stephan Hermlin had noted in 1979 during an interview with his West German publisher Klaus Wagenbach: "The Jewish question, which for a number of years was repressed in our country due to the influence of certain developments in other socialist countries — let us say repressed, anything else would be unjust to the GDR, which up to now has behaved honorably in this matter — this Jewish question is today being openly discussed" ("Wo" 400). Hermlin's own statement contained an element of "repression," for the SED's relationship with the Jews had not always been honorable. Peter Honigmann was closer to the truth when he wrote: "The Party leaders always behave as if their relationship to Jews is not at all burdened by the past. But ignoring the problem does not solve it; it leads at most to repression."[14]

Salomea Genin, a long-time Communist who later rediscovered her Jewish heritage, returned her Party book in 1989 to protest the persistent taboo against Judaism — what she called the "great silence surrounding the Jews" (310) — in the GDR, as well as the fact that the commemorations of 1988 had not initiated a dialogue regarding the history of East German Jews. In an autobiographical statement published in the Federal Republic (Genin chose the title "Rückkehr" [Return], thus echoing and responding to Stephan Hermlin's 1981 essay of the same title), Genin describes her unsuccessful attempts in the 1970s to found a Jewish museum in East Berlin and to write a Master's or doctoral thesis on the subject of European Jews. After the Second World War Genin had returned to the GDR from Australian exile. She sought in East Germany that sense of belonging we have noted elsewhere in this study: she thought she could choose her identity, that in the GDR her Jewish background would mean as little to society as it did to her (309). Later she realizes, against her will and with some dismay, that in her chosen land she was a Jew, whether she cared to be or not (312).

Summarizing her life in East Germany, Genin writes:

> Despite all official pronouncements, my experience has been that the leaders of the GDR are basically suspicious of the Jews, many of whom are independent thinkers.[15] Anti-Semitism, which was always present among the general population, continues. Since 1945 many people have repressed it along with their guilt and their guilt feelings . . . . Despite the "commemoration epidemic" in 1988 and the new consciousness that there are Jews here, there has been no discussion of the past silence. (325)

"Silence, "taboo," and "repression" are words that recur in any critical discussion of Jews in the GDR. As we shall see in the next chapter, writers and filmmakers proved best able to interrogate and revise East German Holocaust discourse and with it the silences and taboos surrounding the "Jewish Question." Indeed, Heinz Knobloch structures his 1979 biography of the Jewish-German Enlightenment thinker Moses Mendelssohn, *Herr Moses in Berlin*, with an archeological metaphor, a metaphor used as well by Freud and Benjamin to signify the excavation of a repressed past.

This repression did not only apply to the government discourse but to that maintained by Jews as well, who contributed to the construction of the East German master narrative.[16] Out of a complicated mixture of motives (depending on the individual they might include a belief in Marxism, suspicion of the Federal Republic, suspicion of Germans in general, support for the GDR as the better Germany, fear of the police state, fear of what might happen if the state collapsed), Jews in the GDR proved among the most politically orthodox East German citizens, although the privileged/protected status of later years meant avoiding contact with Israel (Kessler 163; Kirchner, "Die jüdische" 29) and occasionally being pressured — as in 1967 — to condemn it.[17] By accepting these and other restrictions, writes Jeffrey M. Peck, East German Jews "knew and yet often didn't want to admit how compromised they had become" (Borneman 273).

Party members of Jewish descent (Salomea Genin, for example) treated their Judaism as any other religion, one that they could shed at will. In that they continued the German Enlightenment project of assimilation, as well as the related Marxist-Enlightenment belief in the necessity of leaving religion behind on the road to tolerance. Hitler and Stalin rendered those projects problematic, as East German author Jurek Becker repeatedly demonstrated in his work. Yet many East German Communists of Jewish descent carried on the fragile German-Jewish symbiosis as if there had been no Hitler or Stalin. Sonja Combe, who interviewed some, found them "pathetic, stubborn, and mired in an anachronistic point of view" (140). According to Combe, these people suppressed their Judaism behind a wall of political orthodoxy; what she terms "Jewish identity" could erupt after she turned off the tape recorder (142) or after she struck a nerve, usually in connection with the Holocaust.[18] For the sake of the Party these people returned to the house of the hangman where, often enough, their families had died. The Party repaid some with anti-Semitic purges in the 1950s; those who survived the purges with their careers intact served as mouthpieces for the anti-Zionist, anti-Israeli policies of the SED. Albert Norden, the man in charge of East Germany's anti-Israeli agitation, was the son of a rabbi. Herf writes: "The entry or, as the case may be, re-entry ticket into the East German political elite for those Jews who remained, or recovered prominent positions, in the SED, such as Albert Norden and, after a while, Alexander Abusch, entailed saying little or nothing publicly about the murder of European Jewry. It also meant accepting without protest the diplomatic attacks of the Soviet bloc on Israel and focusing antifascist energies on attacking developments in West Germany."[19] Yet the conviction that these people were German Communists, not Jews, could not even be maintained by the Party. A declaration in the 9 June 1967 issue of *Neues Deutschland* condemns Israel and is signed, not by members of the East German Jewish Community (all of whom refused), but rather by SED members of Jewish descent who in general considered themselves assimilated. The headline nonetheless proclaims the text to be the "Declaration of Jewish Citizens of the GDR."

The children of those determinedly non-Jewish antifascists, children who reemigrated to Germany with their parents or who were born in the GDR, provide "one of the most fascinating aspects of German-Jewish contemporary history," writes Frank Stern (69). These young people redefined their Jewish identity in response to the crisis and collapse of East Germany. Some emigrated; some joined the Jewish Community or "We for Us." Those who grew up in SED families began to confront the silence and taboos of their parents. Stern comments:

> The fact of having been Jewish without being a member of the Jewish congregations in the decades from 1953 to the late 1980s is now an issue in the individual reconstruction of life histories. When considering these recollections and in discussions with members of this postwar generation, it is not easy to tell which aspect had a more subversive character: their Jewishness or their antifascism, as inaccurate and incoherent as both may have been. "Perhaps," it is said, "it was an illusion to believe that one can be German and Jewish." (Stern 69–70)

For our purposes it is important to note that these newcomers, ranging in age from roughly twenty-five to fifty, problematized the signifier "Jewish" in East Germany.[20] Only about 15% ultimately joined the East Berlin Jewish Community. For some, the narrowly religious orientation and orthodox requirements were a determent (many from the group were not halakic Jews); for others, their continuing Communist commitment prevented that step (Kaplan 96–97). Yet this secular group felt itself in some way Jewish. That acknowledgment broke the agreement, long functioning in East Germany — and before that in German-Jewish assimilationist circles — that a Jew was someone who belonged to the Jewish Community.

Regardless of what measure one utilized, at the end of the GDR there were few Jews in that land. Historian Peter Gay, among others, has pointed out that hatred of Jews can thrive even without Jews, and in the later 1980s a number of anti-Semitic incidents in East Germany received widespread attention (for instance, Deutschkron 467). Although attitudes are difficult to quantify, a secret study by the East Berlin Humboldt University claimed that 10% of East German youth sympathized with fascist ideas.[21] Hans Noll asserted: "This anti-Semitism is not, as East German leaders like to portray it, an anachronism, a residue from Nazi times, or a spillover from the Federal Republic; this anti-Semitism is an achievement of East German socialism, where one wanted to repress the Jewish question with coercion" (776). This is what the second *Volkskammer* apology is about. The repression of Judaism in the GDR created an atmosphere of ignorance, one which nourished anti-Semitism, for, as Bebel noted, anti-Semitism is the socialism of fools. Bebel's bon mot received confirmation after 1989 when anti-Semites defaced Bertolt Brecht's gravestone in the eastern part of Berlin. Brecht was not of Jewish descent, though his wife Helene Weigel was; the vandals left her grave untouched.

Notes

[1] Eschwege, "Die jüdische" 74–75; Thompson 102–07. See also Goschler and Schüler.

[2] Cited in Muhlen 200. Burgauer also cites this 177–78. Muhlen claims that the assignment was originally given to Arnold Zweig but was withdrawn when the editor learned he was Jewish. See also Herf, *Divided* 116; 157–58.

[3] Thompson 120. For a survivor's account, see Rapoport.

[4] For more on Zuckermann, see Herf, *Divided*, especially 120–125.

[5] For more on Meyer, see Herf, *Divided*, especially 132–35.

[6] Thompson 84 (synagogue), 146 (geriatric home). Thompson also writes, however, that East German bakeries were prohibited from producing *matzoth*, and that a kosher butcher shop as well as a Jewish kindergarten were closed (136–37).

[7] Hermlin asserted in an interview with *Der Spiegel*: "Ich mache Sie darauf aufmerksam, daß unter allen Volksdemokratien die DDR der einzige Staat war, der sich den Anweisungen Berijas widersetzte." In: "Wir brauchen vor allem Glasnost" *Der Spiegel* 43.6 (1988) 77. See also Eschwege: "Inge Deutschkron glaubt wohl zu Recht, daß die SED-Führung sich verpflichtet fühlte, die gleiche politische Einstellung einzunehmen wie die Regierung der Sowjetunion, deren Vertreter ja damals alle DDR-Instanzen lenkten und leiteten. Und doch behandelte die SED-Führung die Juden weit anständiger und menschlicher als andere sozialistische Regierungen in jenen Jahren. Angemerkt sei, daß dies auch heute noch so ist" ("Die jüdische" 80). Thompson writes: " . . . the D.D.R. purges coincided with similar purges in Hungary, Bulgaria, and Czechoslovakia. One essential difference existed in the D.D.R., the D.D.T. [sic] did not have a theatrical rigged trial or the fulfillment of a death sentence" (155).

[8] For more on Abusch, see Herf, *Divided* 116–120.

[9] Dieckmann writes: "Stand er unter Heldendruck? Welche Schutznöte bedrängten ihn, den Juden, in der frühen DDR? " (*Die Zeit*, 1 Nov. 1996; overseas ed.). For years Hermlin made false claims about his autobiography, for example, that he had been interned in Sachsenhausen and that his father had died there. He also appears to have "de-Judaicized" his family. See Corino; also "Schwere Kämpfe" and "Des Dichters 'wahre Lügen'" in *Der Spiegel*, 7 Oct. 1996. Fritz Raddatz dismisses the speculation of blackmail in *Die Zeit*, 25 Oct. 1996, overseas ed.

[10] Ostow, *Jews* 146. See also Herf, *Divided* 160–61: "The winter purge of 1952–53 constituted the decisive and irrevocable turning point in the history of the regime regarding Jewish matters and the politics of memory in East Germany. With some minor modifications in the 1980s, none of the basic choices of these months and years were fundamentally revised."

[11] See for example the report on a speech by Aris: "Antisemitismus ist in unserer Republik für immer beseitigt," *Neues Deutschland* 17/18 January 1987.

[12] See also Timm, "Israel"; Mertens, "Staatlich"; and Herf, *Divided.*

[13] Serge Schmemann, "In a Tiny Outpost of Judaism, a Rabbi walks Out" *New York Times* 5 May 1988, p. 4. For additional views on Neuman's controversial visit, see Mertens, "Schwindende" 155–159; Ostow, *Jews* 149–154; and Merrit 184–87.

[14] P. Honigmann 110. See also 119.

[15] See also Wolf Biermann's statement: "There was no open hatred of Jews in the GDR, but there did exist a subcutaneous form of anti-Semitism. The apparatschiks' distrust of Jews and the fear of their cosmopolitanism were always at work in the minds of the Bolshevist party line-toers" (104).

[16] See Combe, Borneman and Peck, Herzberg, Ostow, and Wroblewsky for interviews with East German Jews.

[17] Kessler 166. The pressure on Jewish leaders began much earlier. In 1953, writes Herf, East German "Jewish leaders had decided to flee when, following the Slánský trial, the SED Central Committee demanded that they denounce the restitution agreement between West Germany and Israel of fall 1952 and agree to state publicly that the Joint Distribution Committee, which had been assisting Jewish survivors in postwar Europe, was a tool of American espionage; that Zionism was the same as fascism, and Israeli president David Ben-Gurion was an agent of American imperialism; that American justice was criminal because it had condemned the Rosenbergs to death; and that restitution for the injustice done to the Jews amounted to exploitation of the German people" (Herf, *Divided* 133–34).

[18] Combe 145. Compare with Wolf Biermann's anecdote about an East German of Jewish descent who, in Biermann's description, wanted to "be anything, just not Jewish" (105–109).

[19] Herf, "East German" 19. See also Biermann 105 and Giordano 226. O'Doherty challenges such assumptions, but his general attitude that the East German government was "almost entirely altruistic" and "genuinely benevolent" towards Jews, and that it "must be given the benefit of the doubt as to its motives," completely overlooks the instrumentalization of

the "Jewish Question" in East German discourse (*The Portrayal* 13–14; 59–60).

[20] This process is not limited by generation. In the 1990s Wolf Biermann (born in 1936) wrote: "I am not Jewish and I have always been Jewish. The fissure runs straight down the middle" (112).

[21] Deutschkron 458. A West German study of East German youth conducted just before unification found that East German youth displayed, more strongly than their counterparts in the West, characteristics of an "authoritarian personality." The differences were particularly pronounced regarding attitudes towards foreigners: 64.5% of East German youths surveyed thought Germans were better than Turks, while 22.3% of West German youths thought the same; regarding Poles the numbers were 67.3% and 18.6%, regarding Israelis 65.4% and 13.9%, and regarding Congolese 55% and 16.6% (Lederer 590–592). On the other hand, in January 1992 *Der Spiegel* published an EMNID poll with results surprising to some (e.g., Benz, "Antisemitismus" 36; Elsässer 76). According to *Der Spiegel*, 16% of western Germans were classified as possessing anti-Semitic tendencies, as opposed to 4% of eastern Germans. I am wary of such quantification: respondents are often less than honest, and especially eastern Germans had long practice in concealing their true opinions. Furthermore, both Lederer and EMNID operated with questionnaires prepared for West Germans, and it is not clear whether such strategies can be applied without modification to former East Germans. Regarding the EMNID poll, Julius H. Schoeps and Dietmar Sturzbacher argue that if one includes the field of anti-Zionism, then the difference between eastern and western Germans becomes one of quality, not quantity (8). It is in any event true that since 1989 right-wing radicalism has developed very rapidly in eastern Germany, and at a disproportionate rate to western Germany. (*Der Spiegel* 22 July 1996). Whether that results from the continuation of East German thought structures, as some would have it (e.g., Noll 776; P. Fischer 75–79; Kahane 132), or whether it represents a new phenomenon, one occasioned by the dislocations of unification (Titze 10), remains unclear. See also Elsässer 68–80.

4: Berlin, Moscow, and the Imagined Jerusalem: The Holocaust in East German Literature and Film

Was there something in this world that could not be explained according to Marxist categories?

Carl Jakob Danzinger

In his book of 1997, *The Portrayal of Jews in GDR Prose Fiction*, Paul O'Doherty surveys East German literary history and discusses selected works in order to demonstrate a plenitude of "Jewish" issues and themes. O'Doherty's extensive treatment, combined with a yet more comprehensive bibliography that includes East German translations of non-German literature with "Jewish" themes, indicates that the discussion of such themes was hardly taboo in the GDR. Furthermore, that discussion assumed many forms.

O'Doherty's work helps eliminate a recurring blind spot in discussions of Jews and East Germany, especially in the literary sphere. For example, in an article tracing the description of Jews in post-Second World War German literature, Ruth Angress spoke of "Germany," the "German cultural scene," and "German post-Holocaust fiction," but she in general discussed the Federal Republic; she took merely one example, Bruno Apitz's *Nackt unter Wölfen*, from East Germany. Heidi Müller's *Die Judendarstellung in der deutschsprachigen Erzählprosa (1945–1981)* (The Depiction of Jews in German-Language Narrative Prose, 1945–1981) examines only works by non-Jewish authors and hence omits numerous important East German writers. *Jews and Germans since the Holocaust*, a book edited by Anson Rabinbach and Jack Zipes, discusses, despite its title, only West German Jews; such approaches remained fairly standard until the mid 1980s.[1]

In a sense, however, O'Doherty sets up a straw man, for one would assume that a cultural sphere formed extensively by such artists of Jewish descent as Jurek Becker, Wolf Biermann, Stephan

Hermlin, Stefan Heym, Günter Kunert, Kurt Maetzig, Anna Seghers, Fred Wander, Friedrich Wolf, Konrad Wolf, and Arnold Zweig would in some fashion include discussions of "Jewish" themes. Furthermore, O'Doherty appears to believe that the mere presence of such themes demonstrates ipso facto that East Germany was not an anti-Semitic state.[2] Yet even those former East German citizens, for example Chaim Noll or Salomea Genin, who perceived anti-Semitic elements in their country and who spoke of a repression of the "Jewish question," did not mean that "Jewish" issues were not present in East German discourse, but that the discourse itself stipulated the rather limited parameters of discussion. Peter Honig-mann's dictum that one could concern oneself in the GDR with "Jewish" issues, providing one treated them as matter belonging to the past, characterizes the vast majority of East German cultural works. The question is not whether discourse on Jews existed, but rather how it was articulated. Here I agree with the eastern German scholar Thomas Jung that "the representation of both the Holocaust and the Jew . . . is embedded in a specific political-ideological dis-course that instrumentalizes the Jew" (1).

In this chapter I examine Holocaust discourse as generated by East German literature and film. My intention is not so much an in-vestigation of "Jewish" themes or of cultural constructions of Jews — although these matters are of course imbricated — but rather to provide the first overview, in English or in German, of East German cultural responses to the Holocaust. Those responses return over and again to issues of passivity and resistance, otherness and to-getherness. They purport to uncover the causes of anti-Semitism, and they excoriate the failures of postwar West Germany and its al-lies. While extensive, my survey cannot pretend to be comprehen-sive.[3] I have attempted to discuss, at least briefly, paradigmatic works while citing other works in support of my central contention: that in concert with politicians and historians, East German artists con-structed a discourse that served to remember the Holocaust in ways that legitimized the GDR. At the same time, from within works that participated in a state-supporting, antifascist Holocaust discourse, East German writers and filmmakers not infrequently interrogated, extended, and even undermined that very discourse.

As we have seen earlier in this study, the East Germans main-tained official explanations for anti-Semitism and for Nazi racial per-secution. Such explanations emphasized economic criteria and, not incidentally, allowed the socialist GDR to claim that while it had eradicated anti-Semitism, or at least its roots, the capitalist Federal Republic, with its unmastered past, had not. In the 1950s and 1960s many East German artists advanced variants on the economic theory of anti-Semitism; in the later decades, however, they began to question the oversimplifications, contradictions, and self-aggrandizement characterizing that position. Yet always, from the days of the Soviet Occupation Zone, the exigencies of artistic form sometimes allowed for more multiplicitous discourses, even if unintended by the artists themselves.

Let us look first at the fashion in which cultural discourses dovetailed with the East German master narrative of the Holocaust, a narrative by which they were shaped and helped shape. Probably the most authoritative voice in the formation of East German Holocaust discourse in the cultural realm was not that of a Brecht or a Seghers, but rather that of Friedrich Wolf. A German Communist of Jewish descent, Wolf spent the Second World War in Moscow exile, where he published his play *Professor Mamlock* in 1934. Wolf's conventional play tells the story of the prosperous German-Jewish physician Mamlock, a First World War veteran who cannot understand or cope with the degradation to which he is exposed under the Nazis. Mamlock declares that the greatest crime is not to fight when one must fight, but he nonetheless commits suicide, an act the play refuses to accept as resistance. Dying, the doctor recognizes that his path was the wrong one, and he recommends that we follow the correct path chosen by his Communist son.

The conservative Dr. Mamlock finds a number of things to admire in the Nazis whom, it is hinted, he might have in fact supported had they not turned on him.[4] Mamlock's son, who sees things more clearly (22), knows that to understand the Nazis one must understand class conflict (25). The example of the son and his comrades demonstrates that the Communists are in fact worse off than the Jews — which was true in 1934.

An afterword by Wilfried Adling to the paperback East German edition of *Professor Mamlock* applauds the author for demonstrating the connection of race with economics and for utilizing the former as an opportunity to present a thorough analysis of class conflict in bourgeois society. Adling also hails Wolf for his depiction of Communist leadership in the struggle against Hitler, notes that Dr. Mamlock's principles could only have been defended had he been like the Communists and joined them in their struggle, and adds that today, in West Germany, many people face the same choice as Mamlock.

Wolf's play and Adling's analysis present central elements in an orthodox East German artistic confrontation with the Holocaust (that the play had been written before the Holocaust and the GDR merely serves to heighten its ideological validity). Those elements recur and echo in other East German art works as well, in part due to the authoritative presence of Wolf's play in East German cultural life.[5] After *Nathan der Weise*, it was the first play produced in the Soviet Occupation Zone following the Second World War. Printed in large editions, it was required reading in the schools, where it was supposed to offset the otherwise minimal time spent studying the persecution of the Jews (Burgauer 200). (Another text used by East German schools was Brecht's *Furcht und Elend des Dritten Reiches*, [Fear and Misery of the Third Reich, 1938], in which the Jewish Woman, married to a doctor, cannot comprehend what is happening to her. "I never got mixed up in politics. Was I for Thälmann? I'm one of these bourgeois women, who have servants, etc., and now all of a sudden only the blondes are allowed to do that?" [1130]).

In 1960 *Professor Mamlock* was filmed by Friedrich Wolf's son Konrad, one of the most talented filmmakers in the GDR. The film notes in a write-over at the outset: "Friedrich Wolf wrote this drama in 1933. At that time there existed no death camps with six million murdered Jews and war had not broken out yet. The author tell us the story of the German surgeon, of the Jew . . . ." What was for Friedrich Wolf a preliminary diagnosis and a call to arms becomes, with its inclusion in the East German canon, instrumentalized into a justification of the SED dictatorship and a remonstration with those Jews who, by not joining the Communists, must carry some of the blame for the death camps.[6] (Adling's afterword to the East German paperback carries the same message). Mamlock repeatedly declares that there is no worse crime than not to fight when one should, and the adage is carried on a write-over that concludes the film. It serves as a response to the opening write-over, and effectively criminalizes those (bourgeois) Jews such as Mamlock whose resistance took a different form than that offered by the Communists. The DEFA film

Ehe im Schatten (Marriage in the Shadow, 1947), which ends with the double suicide, during the Nazi period, of an unpolitical actor and his Jewish wife, conveys a similar theme, as does Holocaust survivor Peter Edel's novel from 1969, *Die Bilder des Zeugen Schattmann* (The Pictures of Witness Schattmann).[7]

East German literature and film followed closely Friedrich Wolf's script for solidarity, with Communists playing a protective, nurturing, leadership role for the Jews. In his early East German story "Die Zeit der Gemeinsamkeit" (The Time Together, 1949) Stephan Hermlin specifically rejects a Zionist alternative, for his Polish-Jewish-Communist protagonist Mlotek emigrates to Palestine, where he encounters numerous political difficulties and is deported. He then travels to Warsaw, where he helps lead the 1943 revolt in the Jewish ghetto and argues that the Zionists are on the same side as the Nazis (O'Doherty, *Portrayal* 96–97). Hermlin makes references to the Macabees ("Mlotek," like "Macabee," signifies "hammer" or "hammer-like") and to Bar Kochba, the Jewish slave who led a Jewish uprising against Hadrian. As Christiane Schmelzkopf points out, the Macabees and Bar Kochba fought for Jewish political and religious independence, but Hermlin's Mlotek fights, together with non-Jews, for a socialist world (the model is the Soviet Union) in which Jew and non-Jew maintain equal rights. Hermlin's solution renders a Jewish state in Palestine, which in a non-socialist world would in any case represent but an illusory alternative, superfluous (Schmelzkopf 37–39).

Hermlin utilizes a similar approach in *Die erste Reihe* (The Front Rank, 1951), his book of resistance portraits. In keeping with the East German commemoration of the Communist-led antifascist resistance, Hermlin devotes only two of thirty portraits to people of Jewish descent, and he emphasizes not their Jewishness, but their Communism. Young Rudi Arndt, we learn, follows the false path (*Irrweg*) of Zionism, but can correct that by joining the Communist Party (41–42). Writing of the Herbert Baum resistance group, the narrator asserts that Nazi atrocities against the Jews were an obfuscation designed to distract the Jews from the reality of things: "[The fascists wanted the young Jews to see] the world the way it isn't: divided into Jews and non-Jews. They were not supposed to see it the way it is: consisting of oppressors and oppressed, exploiters and exploited." (160) With a hint of condescension, the narrator adds: "Herbert Baum explained patiently [to the Jews] that fascism was not directed against them alone, that anti-Semitism was a devilish maneuver designed to blind exploited people of all nations and races, designed to make them unable to recognize their true enemies, the exploiters" (162). The chapter describes the development of the Baum resistance group which, though of Jewish origin, also contained non-Jewish Communists. Hermlin's narrator maintains an attitude which the former East German scholar Hans Mayer found widespread among leftists at that time, an attitude that emphasized common interests and togetherness (hence the title of Hermlin's narrative of the Warsaw Ghetto uprising), and which dismissed the suggestion of differences between Jewish and Gentile Socialists or Communists as bourgeois prejudice and also as undignified (Schultz 257). Mayer adds however: "The anti-Semitism of Stalin and others could not simply be abolished by decree. To be sure, I recognized this rather late, after two world wars and during my horrified observation of Stalin's anti-Semitic show trials in Moscow and Prague, Sofia and Budapest" (Schultz 257). One of the painful ironies of Hermlin's "Die Zeit der Gemeinsamkeit" and *Die erste Reihe* is that these books, which argue against Zionism and confidently assume that anti-Semitism will disappear under socialism, appeared during a period of growing anti-Semitic activity in East bloc countries. Anti-Semitism did not disappear, but in a sense the Jews did: the memorial erected to Herbert Baum's group opposite the parliament building in East Berlin mentions Communism but not Judaism. And until the 1980s East German schoolbooks did not mention Baum's Jewish background (Ostow, "Persecution" 7–8).

Like Hermlin's Mlotek, novelist Arnold Zweig also experienced a disillusionment with Zionism after spending almost fifteen years in Palestinian exile, and Zweig angered many in the West when, after taking up residence in East Berlin during 1948, he refused to condemn the so-called anti-Zionist campaign in the East bloc. Studying the various versions of Zweig's novel *Die Feuerpause* (Shooting Pause, 1954), Geoffrey V. Davis notes that Zweig gradually diluted or eliminated many references to Judaism: "The Jewish problem becomes part of a much more widespread problem of social injustice, and Jews are, like others, the victims of class justice" (87). Davis also notes that Zweig's earlier work dealing with Jews was not reprinted in the GDR (52–53).

In *Traum ist teuer* (The Dream Is Dear, 1961), Zweig's final published novel, the protagonist's wife Hella refuses, in 1933, to follow him from Austria into Palestinian exile, asserting that there was but one hope for the Jews, and that is to blend into the melting pot of the socialist movement (38). The narrator, who in retrospect calls himself a fool, had believed that building a Jewish state in Palestine could be a progressive project modeled on the Soviet experiment (39). The novel thematizes the many contradictions of Jewish nationalism, and the narrator realizes at the conclusion that his hope of a classless society in Palestine most probably constituted yet another of his "dear dreams." Other books from anti-Zionist authors of Jewish descent, for example Walter Kaufmann's *Drei Reisen ins Gelobte Land* (Three Journeys to the Promised Land, 1980) or Rudolf Hirsch's *Patria Israel* (1983), served similar purposes. Jan Koplowitz's novel *"Bohemia" — Mein Schicksal* ("Bohemia" — My Fate, 1979)[8] begins with a poem by Erich Fried that compares Israel with Nazi Germany.[9]

   In 1958 concentration camp survivor Bruno Apitz published *Nackt unter Wölfen*, a novel about Buchenwald that would become the classic East German contribution to the concentration camp genre. The book celebrates Communist-led resistance at Buchenwald, and tells the story, based on a real incident, of a young Jew whom the Communists hide and ultimately save. It also provides a paradigmatic example of anti-Semitism as a peripheral phenomenon, one subordinate to class struggle. Peter Demetz reads the novel within the strictures of the concentration camp genre established by such writers as Anna Seghers or Wolfgang Langhoff, who wrote before the full implications of the mass deportations or the Final Solution were known (26). (This is to some extent true, but Apitz was writing over ten years later than Langhoff or Seghers.) "The genre reflected the experience of Communists and, in some instance, the formal restrictions established by their Party: The persecuted were seen in terms of class and party allegiances, and the genre itself was unwilling to perceive them as loyal or assimilated members of a religious and ethnic community" (26). Demetz notes that the Polish Jew who smuggles the Jewish child into Buchenwald is only once referred to as a Jew, and that the prisoners prefer to speak of the child as Polish, not Jewish. Apitz even alters the name of the child to make it sound less Jewish (Demetz 27). The French critic Jean-Paul Bier writes that the child's Jewishness appears incidental, and that Auschwitz remains a peripheral motif (188). As we noted in Chapter 2, Ruth Angress is more critical: "The Jew as victim of the Holocaust is literally infantilized, and put into the shadow by the Comrades, as if Jews had been only incidental victims compared to the genuine, ideological enemy who preserved his integrity and knew how to fight back" (216). The recent publication of documents by Lutz Niethammer demonstrates at what price the Communists preserved their integrity at Buchenwald: by cooperating with the Nazis and helping to decide which inmates would be murdered. Niethammer believes the victims included non-ideological Jews (55).

Frank Beyer's 1963 film of Apitz's novel, though a more satisfying work aesthetically, does not depart from the principal political message and thus preserves the condescending attitude that we have also traced in East German concentration camp memorial exhibitions regarding Jews or Sinti and Roma. One sees the same constraints in drama, where, as Anat Feinberg asserts, Jewish victims are in general secondary figures. Feinberg writes: "The Jew that one occasionally finds in East German drama does not represent his or her own fate, or even that of the Jews, but rather in the majority of cases that of collective suffering under the Nazi regime" (74). An exemplary work is Hedda Zinner's *Ravensbrücker Ballade* (Ravensbrück Ballad, 1961), set in Ravensbrück. The Jewish Lea clearly plays a less important role than her political comrades, though in surrealistic choruses she serves as a figure for all victims of fascism. Yet even this reserved rendering caused problems as late as 1985 in the GDR, when a television version was abruptly discontinued at the wish of the Committee of Antifascist Resistance Fighters (Jarmartz 74). Zinner was informed that the play contained too many "asocial" characters, which reduced the heroism of the political prisoners (Zinner, "Legitimer" 194).

Rolf Schneider's *Geschichte von Moischele* (Moischele's Story, written 1964–65) presents a particularly egregious example of the condescension inherent in standard East German responses to the Holocaust. The play narrates the story of the Jewish boy Moischele from his childhood in a Polish village through his persecution in the Second World War. After the war he works as a racketeer in Berlin, and is as a result imprisoned in an East German "reeducation camp" for juveniles. The text contrasts Moischele, who exemplifies most stereotypical anti-Semitic traits (including the "mauscheln" that Sander Gilman and Ruth Angress have acutely discussed), with the non-Jewish German, Joseph. Originally an anti-Communist, anti-Semitic anarchist, Joseph is so moved by the example of Communist resistance and heroism during the war that he himself becomes a Communist eager to help build the GDR. In the final scene he confronts Moischele and a former Hitler Youth leader (the Jew Moischele is suggesting to the Nazi that they work together to develop shady schemes) in a youth reeducation facility. The play's final lines, spoken to the Jew, come from the Communist: "I am your educator" (277).

Jews needed to be educated. Brecht made his contribution, as did Herbert Baum and Schneider's Joseph. Peter Edel, an East German Communist of Jewish descent, writes in his autobiographical novel *Die Bilder des Zeugen Schattmann* of Helmut Wall, a Communist without prejudice (300), who, like Herbert Baum, patiently explains the basics of class struggle to the Jews (291). The East German author Walter Kaufmann, of Jewish descent, begins his anti-Zionist *Drei Reisen ins Gelobte Land* with a quote from writer Louis Fürnberg that makes the same gesture:

> I am myself too deeply and too good a Jew to be able to remain quiet when I see the crimes that the Jewish bourgeoisie continually commits against the Jewish masses. But the tendency of the Jewish masses to believe the Jewish bourgeoisie, and not us Marxists, can simply not be changed . . . . What, I ask myself, do the Jews matter to me? Because I am one myself, I have a kind of personal interest in seeing their tragedy end. Can it end otherwise than on the path that we show the Jews?

The right path is that of Rudi Arndt, Herbert Baum, Peter Edel, and Walter Kaufmann — the path taken by Mamlock's (Jewish)-Communist son.

Elsewhere in East German Holocaust discourse we have traced an effort to demonize the West German state and to hallow the East German one. Such efforts climaxed during the Eichmann trial and included East German cultural products. *Jetzt und in der Stunde meines Todes* (Now and in the Hour of My Death) a DEFA entertainment film of 1964, takes place in West Berlin with the Eichmann trial in Jerusalem as backdrop. Patterned on the fast-paced Hollywood detective genre, Konrad Petzold's film presents an array of conspiracies, murders, and former Nazis turned postwar Mafiosi. The gangsters are working for West Germans compromised by

Eichmann's testimony. Those who try to discern the truth — a young policeman and a young reporter — are both removed from the case by their superiors. The reporter's editor withdraws support after a threatening phone conversation that reminds him of the Nazi period — the caller utilizes the term "Jewish pig" and threatens him with financial ruin. The reporter, who continues to work on her own, is murdered. Hence when a television broadcast announces that, cursed by the world, Eichmann has been hanged, we understand that powerful West Germans are clearly out of step with the rest of the world.

The Eichmann trial gave East German attacks on the Federal Republic additional publicity, but the campaign had begun earlier. In a 1958 documentary entitled *Ein Tagebuch für Anne Frank* (A Diary for Anne Frank), the directors summarily detail who Frank was and the process of her deportation (to work for German industry) and murder (with gas supplied by German corporations). The film briefly depicts the liberation of the camps and a British military tribunal, asserting that a few Nazi criminals were hanged, but that most were freed into West Germany. The hidden camera then shows former Nazis as respected West German citizens while the narrator provides their addresses. Most of the film is dedicated to such methods, and Anne Frank's story is lost in it, though the film returns to her at the end: "You were the victim — the murderers still live. For you the horror was nameless — for us it has a name. We know the murderers would do the same if they could."[10]

"If there had been no Globke, there could have been no Eichmann" is the message of *Aktion J* (1961), a pseudo-documentary exposé of Globke's career. A historical overview of Hitler's rise emphasizes that Communists had warned the German people about the Nazis, and that Communists had been the true defenders of human rights. The film argues that capitalist monopolies brought Hitler to power and that their main enemy was the working class. "But always when the working class suffers, other oppressed groups suffer too. In this case primarily the Jews." The film quotes a Nazi as claiming "if there were no Jews we would have had to invent them" in order to emphasize the fascists' diversionary tactics.

Juxtaposing pictures and speeches of West German Chancellor Adenauer and Goebbels, or superimposing a picture of Hitler on Adenauer, the film signals the continuity of the past. "As long as the Globkes rule in Bonn, Aktion J is still in action." The narrator emphasizes however that Globke's power stops "in the middle [sic] of Germany, in the GDR." The film concludes with propaganda pictures celebrating East Germany. The documentary film *Mord in Lwow* (Murder in Lvov, 1960) proceeds in the same fashion, although it is directed at Theodor Oberländer, a former Nazi who served for seven years as West Germany's Secretary of All-German Affairs. The image of dead Jews being bulldozed into mass graves, accompanied by the near hysterical voice of the narrator, Hewart Grosse, demonizing West Germany, provides a particularly tasteless setting to this film which concludes by asserting "Oberländer, that is the [Bonn] regime." The first postwar German feature film, one produced in the Soviet Occupation Zone, carried the programmatic title *Die Mörder sind unter uns* (The Murderers Are among Us, 1946). Fourteen years later *Mord in Lwow* features East Germans carrying placards addressed to West Germans: "Die Mörder sind unter euch!" (The murderers are among you!).

Two plays from this time — Herbert Keller's *Begegnung 57* (Meeting 57, 1958) and Fritz Kuhn's *Kredit bei Nibelungen* (Credit from the Nibelungs, 1960) — attack West Germany as the refuge of former, current, and future Nazis, as the Germany where anti-Semitism continues unabated and the past repeats itself. Several DEFA feature films proclaimed the same message. *Zwischenfall in Benderath* (Incident in Benderath), a film of 1956, is set in a small West German city called Benderath. A high school teacher, Päker, characterizes the Jewish pupil Jakob Lewin as a "cowardly Oriental" and a "state enemy" (the latter term often used by Eastern European governments just previous to that time). Jakob's schoolmates and their parents support Jakob, and the teacher must apologize before being transferred to another school.

Jakob's teacher slurs him with racial epithets, but his real motivation during this film set in 1955 is political. Päker's actual target is Jakob's father, a Communist who publicly opposes West German rearmament and integration into NATO. The teacher, who advocates rearmament at political rallies of the governing party, participates in a wide-ranging conspiracy that includes the highest levels of the West German government. Although Päker must be transferred, his handlers assure him that they have other important tasks for him and that Jakob's family will continue to suffer. As the local orchestra plays Liszt's *Les Préludes* (used by the Nazis to preface important announcements),[11] Jakob is informed that his father has been arrested.

Jakob's friends, who have supported him, realize that although their ordeal is over, such (Jewish)-Communists as Jakob will need to continue to fight for justice in West Germany.

The film *Der Prozeß wird vertagt* (The Trial Is Postponed, 1958) tells the story of a German Jew, Michael Vierkant, who had emigrated during the Nazi period and who returns as a British citizen to West Germany after the war. He encounters a former Nazi informer who had been responsible for the death of Vierkant's sister. The Nazi, who has meanwhile attained an important government post in West Germany, is accidentally killed by Vierkant during an altercation. Vierkant is arrested, and high-ranking West German government officials (who intend to outlaw the Communist Party) attempt to portray him as a Communist agent. He has the support of Maria Jäger (whose father's writing was banned by the Nazis), the British journalist Crossert (whose newspaper refuses, due to political considerations, to print the truth about Vierkant), and a West German Communist (who briefly shares a cell with him and gives the Jew some sage political advice). His supporters hold an international press conference designed to break the conspiracy of silence maintained by the West German neo-fascists. The East German and Soviet journalists are especially receptive, and the resulting international publicity causes a postponement of the trial.

Similarly, in the film *Chronik eines Mordes* (Chronicle of a Murder, 1965), the Jewish survivor Ruth Bodenheim returns to her home in West Germany. She intends to murder a Nazi named Zwischenzahl, who had been responsible for the massacre of some Jews and the deportation of others (including her parents).[12] Bodenheim had been sent to a German army bordello.[13] The Americans arrest Zwischenzahl, but the man is an industrialist and, making an economic deal with the Americans, he is freed and leaves for exile in South America. He returns after 10 years to run successfully for mayor. Bodenheim possesses documents that incriminate Zwischenzahl, but she can find no West German official willing to help her. During Zwischenzahl's inauguration she murders him. As was the case with Jakob Lewin and Michael Vierkant, Ruth Bodenheim finds herself confronted with an array of powerful West German officials who conspire to protect an unrepentant Nazi. Bodenheim's enemies attempt to silence her through incarceration in a mental hospital, but the District Attorney has been so impressed by her integrity that he changes sides in order to defend her. The outcome is uncertain;

the lawyer tells her she must expect a harsh judgment from the neo-Nazis. The use of the Holocaust to attack the Federal Republic while celebrating the better German state remained a standard element in East German Holocaust discourse until the very end. Peter Edel's novel *Die Bilder des Zeugen Schattmann* (1969), subtitled "A Novel about the German Past and Present," describes in part the East German trial *in absentia* of Globke. *Schüsse in Marienbad* (Shots in Marienbad, 1974) is a Czech/East German detective film in which Czech police track down a Nazi assassin who then escapes to West Germany. The 1989 documentary film *Der Mann an der Rampe* (The Man at the Ramp) condemns West Germany as a Nazi refuge. These various works all construct, rhetorically and/or with images, a primitive parallel between the Federal Republic and Nazi Germany. What Dan Diner asserted in a different context applies here as well: such "over-generalizing defamation of the Federal Republic . . . did little more than trivialize National Socialism."[14]

Although the arch-enemy in East German Holocaust discourse was and remained West Germany, East Germans regularly utilized similar strategies to excoriate Israel and the United States as well. *Welch ein Wort in die Kälte gerufen* (What a Word Shouted into the Cold, 1968), the most extensive collection of Holocaust poetry published in East Germany, appeared soon after the 1967 Arab-Israeli war; its introduction devotes several paragraphs to a discussion of Israeli fascism (Seydel 21–22). That same year Rolf Schneider's play *Prozeß in Nürnberg* (The Nuremberg Trial) targets the United States. Schneider uses the documentary techniques developed by Peter Weiss and others to argue that capitalists brought Hitler to power and profited from his rule. Through his careful editing and compression of the trial transcripts, Schneider places into the mouths of the American, British, and French prosecutors a condemnation of the capitalist elite that the western allies would soon utilize to create and stabilize West Germany. The American prosecutor has the final speech, in which he asserts that the Nuremberg trial has created new laws and new standards to condemn aggression and crimes against humanity. In the future, he declares, the victorious allies will also be judged by these standards. As Schneider remarks darkly after the play, this war crimes tribunal can be repeated. Against the backdrop of the Vietnam war, his message is not dissimilar to the popular West German leftist chant of the time: "SS-SA-USA."

Yet even as the literature and film discussed above helped establish the rather rigid parameters of East German Holocaust discourse (and the Party would, with some slackening, enforce those parameters until 1989), artists in the East produced works of greater complexity as well. Two films from the Soviet Occupation Zone, *Ehe im Schatten* (Marriage in the Shadow) and *Affaire Blum* (The Blum Affair), Willi Bredel's story "Das schweigende Dorf" (The Silent Village, 1948), Martin Gregor-Dellin's novel *Jüdisches Largo* (Jewish Largo, 1956), and *Sterne* (Stars), a film of 1959, resist overt instrumentalization, even if they do not avoid it. That resistance generates productive tensions.

Ehe im Schatten (1947), released in the second year of DEFA by Kurt Maetzig, is dedicated to the actor Joachim Gottschalk, who together with his Jewish wife, Meta Wolff, committed suicide in 1941. The film is based on their story. In 1947, before the appropriation of the Holocaust for the purposes of East German self-legitimization, the double suicide appears as a last possibility of retaining dignity when faced with deportation; indeed, Maetzig's Jewish mother met a similar fate under the Nazis. Nonetheless, the conclusion is not unproblematic. Confronting a Nazi cultural functionary, the husband exclaims that "we [artists] are just as guilty as you. We didn't want to have anything to do with politics." Even in this more inclusive period of postwar antifascism, it is hard not to hear an echo of Mamlock's "false path" in these words.

Maetzig confronts German viewers with the tribulations of Jews in wartime Berlin, focusing on the Jewish wife in a "mixed marriage." The film features the growing fear and the daily humiliations of German Jews against the historical backdrop of the Nuremberg Laws, the so-called *Kristallnacht*, forced labor, arrests and deportations. The Jewish protagonist Elisabeth declares early in the movie that "now our friends will have to step forward," but with the exception of the non-Jewish Hans, who marries her in part to protect her, most do not. The film emphasizes German passivity by numerous images that thematize the gaze. In the opening scene, for example, the camera shows a full theater watching the suicide scene (which foreshadows the later suicides in the movie) from Friedrich Schiller's *Kabale und Liebe* (Intrigue and Love, 1784). The camera not only focuses on the audience, but cuts to actors backstage watching through windows. Later scenes in theaters and cinemas reprise these images, as do frequent other mise-en-scènes utilizing windowpanes or mirrors — the protagonists observe "*Kristallnacht*" through windows. Symbolized by a policeman who does nothing to stop the pogrom, Germans remain passive spectators regarding the Nazis. This includes Jewish-Germans as well, for the assimilated, bourgeois Elisabeth does not leave Germany despite repeated warnings and provocation, nor does she actively resist, depending instead on the protection of her non-Jewish husband. In a curious piece of rhetorical slippage, the characters repeatedly refer to the Nazis as a natural force, a landslide that cannot be stopped. One finds a similarly non-Marxist use of figurative language in East German history writing and in the concentration camp memorials.

Ehe im Schatten was filmed as a melodrama and it reached a large public. (In this respect it anticipates the US television film *Holocaust* from 1978). The film had its premiere in all four sections of Berlin on 4 October 1947, and with over 10 million viewers it was the most successful DEFA film of the 1940s, and one of the most successful ever.

In contrast to the emotion-laden film by Maetzig, Erich Engel's *Affaire Blum* (1948), based on events from 1926–27, utilizes Brechtian distancing techniques that present the viewer with the facts at the outset. A former *Freikorps* thug murders an accountant and, with the assistance of right-wing German nationalist judges and politicians, succeeds in framing the rich Jewish industrialist Blum.[15] Supported by the Left, Blum must ultimately be freed. At the conclusion his non-Jewish wife comforts him with the remarks that they were, after all, living in Germany.

Although it may appear anomalous to find Weimar leftists supporting an industrialist, Jewish or not, the film points out that Blum is a political friend of the Socialist State President Vilshinski, and that he contributes financially to Vilshinski's party. The only overt slur directed against Blum is political: he is accused of being a "good dialectician, a typical trait." The impressive film demonstrates the fashion in which prejudice and political calculation combine to orchestrate a show trial in which an innocent Jew will be made to symbolize the dangerous power of Jewish conspiracy. Soon thereafter the Soviet bloc countries would do just that.

In 1948 Willi Bredel, a German Communist writer who had spent the Second World War in prison, in exile, and as a soldier in the Soviet army, published "Das schweigende Dorf" (The Silent Village). Set in 1947, the story describes a village in the Soviet Occupation Zone that has kept silent regarding a massacre of Jewish women and children during the last days of the war. The government ultimately uncovers the crime and sentences the main perpetrator to twenty years in prison. Beyond that, the narrator comments bitterly, little happens. None of the accomplices are arrested, a planned memorial stone is never erected, and the many well-meaning speeches have no visible effect. The narrator asserts that the incident is almost forgotten, and that the villagers behave as if they had received absolution for their guilt (264).

That twist is somewhat surprising in a story published in the Soviet Occupation Zone, and there are other unusual elements as well. To be sure, Bredel's narrative displays open partisanship with its strongly sympathetic depiction of the Russians. The narrator furthermore mentions a former Nazi who now is earning a fortune in the English Occupation Zone, and another former Nazi flees the Soviet Zone for the West. But the story also includes a former Nazi in the Soviet Zone who had "Aryanized" a Jewish mill and continues to rent it out profitably. (Such subjects would soon become taboo in the GDR). Additionally, four of the five men who help commit the massacre of the Jews are workers or farmers, privileged classes in the "first workers' and farmers' state on German soil," as the East Germans would call their country. Finally, we learn that the narrator's fiancé saves a Jewish child from the massacre and later adopts it. Although Bredel describes the child's features in stereotypical fashion, he depicts the fiancé's action in terms of simple humanity — the protection of the child is not yet instrumentalized as in Bruno Apitz's *Nackt unter Wölfen*. As Paul O'Doherty points out, the Jewish background of the child also represents a source of public pride, an attitude that would soon grow problematic in the GDR.[16] Indeed, as with *Ehe im Schatten*, "Das schweigende Dorf" still frames much of its response to the Holocaust in moral terms. The narrator demands of the villagers: "Don't you understand that all who knew of the crime, but remained silent, made themselves guilty as well?

Don't you know that anyone who spares murderers is also partly guilty of the murder?" (263).

Between 1949 and 1951, a period of increasing Stalinization and "anti-Zionist" agitation in the Soviet bloc, Martin Gregor-Dellin wrote his first novel. It recounts the story of a young German, Jakob Haferglanz, who on account of his Jewish father is increasingly persecuted during the Third Reich. Humiliated and ostracized, Jakob commits suicide. As in *Ehe im Schatten* (and unlike Friedrich Wolf's *Professor Mamlock*), the novel portrays the suicide with empathy; although there is a semi-omniscient narrator, the perspective aligns itself closely with Jakob. The novel features recognizable GDR elements. Although a musical genius, the other-worldly Jakob possesses absolutely no political sophistication. His only friend is from a Communist family, and when the Nazis arrest that family, Jakob is left "alone and lost" (Gregor-Dellin 270). But socialist realist critics objected to the novel's "bourgeois qualities"; that objection, together with East German Jewish persecutions of the early 1950s, prevented publication until 1956. (The publisher imposed the title *Jüdisches Largo*, or Jewish Largo). Two years later the book was withdrawn. In 1963 — by then Gregor-Dellin had left the GDR for the West — the novel was reprinted in the Federal Republic under the title *Jakob Haferglanz.* With its elusive, metaphorical, poetic style and its lack of tendentiousness it stands in marked contrast to most other East German writing on the Holocaust, especially from that period. It represents an artistic direction and strategy the GDR consciously chose not to pursue.

During the period of Stalinist Jewish persecutions in the early 1950s, East German filmmakers avoided Holocaust themes;[17] even Apitz's *Nackt unter Wölfen*, originally conceived as a film, was refused by the East German Babelsberg film studios in 1955 (D. Wolf 257) and could not be filmed until 1963. In the second half of the 1950s filmmakers could return to the subject, provided they instrumentalized it into an attack on West Germany (for instance, *Zwischenfall in Benderath, Der Prozeß wird vertagt, Ein Tagebuch für Anne Frank*). A partial exception in this regard is Konrad Wolf's *Sterne* (Stars, 1959), an East German/Bulgarian production and Wolf's most explicit confrontation with the Holocaust. Set in German-occupied Bulgaria during the Second World War, the film features the encounter of a German soldier (he is given the name "Walter" by the postwar Bulgarian narrator) with the Jewish Ruth from a transport of Greek Jews en route to Auschwitz. His conversation with (and erotic attraction for) the woman changes his life: he plans to free her, and begins to work with the Bulgarian resistance.[18] West Germans objected to the didactic ending, and for them the protagonist's decision to join the partisans had to be cut (Joos 136), but surely other questions raised by the film caused concern. *Sterne* deals, after all, with issues of personal responsibility and with the possibilities of resistance among ordinary German soldiers. Walter, a dreamy painter, holds the Nazis in some disdain and believes himself better than they; he calls his roommate an ape. But soon thereafter Ruth characterizes all Germans, Walter included, as wild animals (the film cuts to a shot of Walter's roommate eating in bestial fashion). When the German protagonist tries to distance himself from a recent action by the German army, Ruth responds: "You are all guilty, guilty in the same way, or are you perhaps without guilt for this act? For everything that has happened in the past years?" For all its primitive woodcut awkwardness (Feinberg 67), Alfred Matusche's play *Der Regenwettermann* (The Rainy Weather Man, 1963 in television, 1965 in theaters), in which a German army soldier commits suicide rather than execute Polish Jews, also attempts to address similar issues. And Hermann Kant's autobiographical *Der Aufenthalt* (The Stop Over, 1977) would later describe the "education" of a young German soldier who, at the end of the Second World War, is falsely accused of having murdered a Polish civilian.[19] Held prisoner by the Poles, the young German begins to understand the magnitude of crimes by the SS and the German army, and his shared responsibility — if in a mediated way — for their savagery. It is worth recalling that the issue of German army guilt, discussed rather early in East German cultural works, remained (and remains) a highly volatile subject in the Federal Republic.[20]

German guilt, especially in eastern Europe, provides the touchstone for Johannes Bobrowski's unique literary opus. Born in 1917 in Tilsit, in what was at that time eastern Germany, Bobrowski grew up in an area inhabited by Germans, Poles, Lithuanians, Sinti and Roma, and Jews. The ethnic and economic tensions between these groups turned genocidal with the arrival of Hitler's army. Bobrowski served as a foot soldier in that army. Much of his subsequent literary work constitutes an act of penance reflecting deep shame for the role of the Germans in the East: "A long history of calamity and guilt, since the days of the Teutonic Order, which stands on my people's account. Not that it can ever be erased or atoned for, but it is worth hope and an honest attempt in German poetry" (Cited in Flores 233). In his life and work Bobrowski proved at once the insider and outsider: a devout Christian living in socialism, he received prestigious literary prizes from both East and West Germany.

In his poetry Bobrowski returned over and again to the eastern European Jewish culture extinguished by the German army. His poem "Traces in the Sand" ("Die Spur im Sand," 1954) is particularly illustrative of this theme:

> The pale old man
> in the faded caftan.
> The old-time earlocks. Aaron,
> I used to know your house.
> You bear its ashes away
> in your shoes.
>
> Your brother drove you from its door. I followed
> you. How your caftan flapped about
> your feet! All I was left were traces
> in the sand.
> Then I sometimes
> saw you of an evening
> coming down
> the lane, whispering.
> With your white hands
> you threw the snow-seed
> over the barn roof.
>
> Because your fathers' god
> will continue to brighten
> the years for us, Aaron,
> traces remain in the dust of the streets,
> I shall find you.
> And go.
> And I bear
> your distance, your expectation
> on my shoulders.[21]

As David Scrase points out in his study of Bobrowski, the use of "ashes" evokes both Paul Celan's famous Holocaust poem "Todesfuge" (Death Fugue) and the pogroms of eastern Europe. The ambiguous lines "I followed/ you" clearly point to a sense of personal responsibility, and the poem's conclusion refers to the duties of a German poet, or perhaps of all Germans (21–22). Bobrowski addresses similar themes in such poems as "Auf den jüdischen Händler A.S." (To the Jewish Dealer A.S., 1954), "Die Heimat des Malers Chagall" (The Homeland of the Painter Chagall, 1954), "Holunderblüte" (Elder-Blossom, 1960), "An den Chassid Barkan" (To the Chassid Barkan, 1960), and in his poetic homages to the German-Jewish poets Gertrud Kolmar, Else Lasker-Schüler, and Nelly Sachs.

Bobrowski's prose, like his poetry, often conjures up (former) Jewish life in the East. "Mäusefest" (Mouse Feast, 1962) describes an encounter between a young German army soldier and a Polish Jew at the outset of the Second World War. "Die ersten beiden Sätze für ein Deutschlandbuch" (The First Two Sentences for a Book about Germany, 1964) satirizes German pleas of ignorance concerning the Holocaust. "Der Tänzer Malige" (Malige the Dancer, 1965), set in Poland at the beginning of the Second World War, demonstrates an example of resistance from within the German army to Nazi anti-Jewish measures.

Levins Mühle (Levin's Mill, 1964), Bobrowski's prose masterwork, takes place in a Polish-German village within Bismarck's nineteenth-century German Reich. The Russian Jew Leo Levin builds a mill that competes with the mill owned by the narrator's German grandfather Johann. Johann destroys Levin's mill, blocks Levin's efforts at legal redress, and eventually drives Levin out of Germany.

Levins Mühle contains Bobrowski's most extensive treatment of anti-Semitism. Grandfather Johann does not hesitate to inflame religious, jingoistic, or xenophobic sentiments to achieve his ends, but his real motivations are economic. The wandering flutist Johann Vladimir Geethe (the name combines that of Goethe with Lenin) tells us the Germans act as they do "because of money" (*Levin's* 174). The narrator does not contradict this opinion, and we may take it as authoritative. For all its formal distance from the techniques of socialist realism, Bobrowski's novel does not depart markedly from the orthodox East German interpretation of anti-Semitism.

This applies yet more so to Horst Seemann's film *Levins Mühle* (1980), which omits some of the religious motivations for anti-Semitism that one finds (to be sure in a subordinate role) in Bobrowski's novel, concentrating on the economic. The conversation about the Germans and money, cited above, is defining in the film.

Seemann's film portrays Levin as victim from the outset: the opening images depict his mill and menorah being washed away while Levin cries. Levin, who in the film is religious and wears a skullcap, is a passive figure who must be assisted by members of other oppressed groups, a "rainbow coalition" of "Gypsies," Slavs from various nations, and outcast Germans. Levin's allies organize a circus, during which they parade in carnivalesque style while chanting a song indicting the Grandfather. Levin does not participate; he watches, and leaves early. The performers represent him symbolically in their parade with a figure wearing whiteface, a skullcap, and bowing his head. The scene is reprised near the conclusion of the film, when Levin's allies, singing the same song, win a barroom brawl with the Germans. Levin remains seated. At the conclusion of the movie he leaves with his "Gypsy" wife for his family in Russia but, in a criticism of Jewish clannishness, they remain outsiders there and leave for a life of wandering.

Johannes Bobrowski was the non-Jewish East German author who most consistently evoked "Jewish" themes and images in his writing. His dark, enigmatic tropes can be deeply moving, but they are not unproblematic. His insistence on the politically suspect word *"Heimat"* has proved troubling to some. Furthermore, as noted above, his Jews remain quite passive: Levin needs the help of a coalition of the oppressed. The Jew in "Mäusefest" knows already in advance of the Holocaust that he will not resist, and the Jews in "Der Tänzer Malige" need the intercession of a German artist. With his metaphors, Bobrowski often suggests that Jews are near magical creatures closely tied to nature: the Jew in "Mäusefest," for example, converses with the moon. Such images help underscore the rootedness of the Jews within the eastern European landscape, and they convey the melancholy sense that the vanished culture continues to inhabit and haunt that landscape. But Bobrowski's language also runs the risk of aestheticizing the eastern Jews into mythological or fairy-tale creatures at a remove from the real, flesh and blood victims of the Nazi army.

As we have noted, Peter Edel's novel *Die Bilder des Zeugen Schatt-mann* rehearses most of the familiar elements in East German Holocaust discourse. Similar to Friedrich Wolf's *Professor Mamlock*, Edel includes as a central figure the assimilated, bourgeois, Jewish doctor Marcus who served in the First World War and is a German humanist. Marcus's class supports the Nazis, if only through a lack of political resistance; the novel makes clear, as the East German literary critic Heinz Lorenz pointed out, that the bourgeois Jews failed politically (133). Marcus's awakening comes too late; his niece Esther and her husband Frank Schattmann can still find the right path. They separate themselves from the religious Jews, who do not resist, and find their way to the Communists, who teach them how to fight.[22] Esther dies in Auschwitz, but Frank survives, and he lives happily as an honored citizen in the GDR. He holds the Federal Republic in great disdain and gives evidence against Globke.

The publication of Jurek Becker's *Jakob der Lügner* (Jakob the Liar) in the same year as Edel's novel, and Fred Wander's *Der siebente Brunnen* (The Seventh Well) in 1971, brought new and rather different voices into East German Holocaust discourse. Like Edel, both Becker and Wander survived concentration camps in which they had been imprisoned as Jews, but unlike Edel, their books serve as correctives to earlier Marxist writing on the subject. Wander's Buchenwald, where some of *Der siebente Brunnen* takes place, is very different from Bruno Apitz's; Wander's narrator, ill with typhus, registers the prisoners' uprising (which forms the optimistic denouement to Apitz's novel) passively, with dream-like images.

Wander's title echoes that of Anna Seghers's *Das siebte Kreuz* (The Seventh Cross, 1944) in which Seghers transforms an empty seventh cross, representing a prisoner who has escaped from a concentration camp and whom the Nazis cannot recapture, into a secular symbol of political hope. Wander's title remains religious. It is taken from the writing of Rabbi Löw (1520–1609), writing that Wander cites as epigram: "The seventh well — water of pureness, freed of all impurities; impervious to pollution and turbidness; of immaculate transparency; ready for future generations, that they might alight from the darkness, their eyes clear, their hearts freed." That, too, constitutes a revision, for in his story "Die Zeit der Gemeinsamkeit," Stephan Hermlin contrasts favorably those Jews who read Lenin with those who seek solace in the "legends of the past," and he specifically cites Rabbi Löw's Golem as one such legend.[23]

Jurek Becker's East German narrator may well be thinking of "Die Zeit der Gemeinsamkeit" or *Nackt unter Wölfen* when he writes:

> I can tell you that I have since read with awe about Warsaw and Buchenwald, another world but comparable. I have read much about heroism, probably too much, I have been gripped by sense-less envy . . . . Be that as it may, we remained passive until the last second, and there's nothing I can do about it. I am not unaware than an oppressed people can only be truly liberated if it contributes towards its liberation, if it goes at least a little bit of the way to meet the Messiah. We did not do this . . . . Where I was, there was no resistance. (*Jakob the Liar* 72–73)

Yet the narrator's own narrative in a sense deconstructs his bow to an East German politics that narrowly defined resistance as armed and Communist-led while depicting non-Communist Jews as passive. Becker's grumpy, fearful Jakob indeed acts heroically; his heroism is not the pathos-strewn, orthodox Communist variety conjured by the narrator above, but is informed rather by a stock of Jewish characters and tropes from a tradition of Jewish storytelling. Jakob's friend Kowalski is also capable of heroism, for he saves Jakob's life at the risk of his own. Most intriguing is the "peripheral" figure of the famous Dr. Kirschbaum, head of a hospital, in great demand as a heart specialist:

> Kirschbaum has never given a thought to being a Jew; his father before him was a surgeon, what does it mean, of Jewish origin, they force you to be a Jew while you yourself have no idea what that really is. Now [in the ghetto] he is surrounded only by Jews, for the first time in his life nothing but Jews. He has racked his brains about them, wanting to find out what it is that they all have in common: in vain, they have nothing recognizable in common, and he most emphatically nothing whatever. (*Jakob the Liar* 59).

Like his literary predecessor Dr. Mamlock, Dr. Kirschbaum is assimilated and unable to comprehend what is being done to him. Like Dr. Mamlock, Kirschbaum dies by suicide — he kills himself rather than treat an SS officer. Yet unlike Mamlock's death, Kirschbaum's can now be seen as a gesture of resistance, as an act that allows the doctor to maintain his dignity and integrity.

Both Becker and Wander swerve, then, from the socialist realist prescription for Communist-led resistance such as one finds with Hermlin or Apitz or Edel.[24] Writing a positive review of *Jakob der Lügner* for the Party paper *Neues Deutschland*, the East German reviewer noted that while reading Becker he felt the need to remember those books that demonstrated how the Party "organized and led the real struggle" (14 May 1969). He adds that Becker's petit bourgeois protagonist does not possess the proper class standpoint and the appropriate political consciousness for such matters.

In de-emphasizing the political, neither book presents the orthodox Marxist view of anti-Semitism. Wander's fiction thus differs from a public letter he wrote to Primo Levi, in which he advances economic arguments as an explanation for anti-Semitism in the Federal Republic. Wander also chided Levi, albeit gently, for "mistakes and subjective, somewhat incomplete observations of the political prisoners" in his work, and for not emphasizing adequately the work of the illegal resistance organizations in the different camps ("Brief" 25). Wander notes that the encounter with political prisoners was decisive for his future development, yet in Wander's autobiographical *Der siebente Brunnen* the French resistance fighter and political prisoner Pépé remains a shadowy figure, and we never really learn how he assists the narrator. Far more important for the narrator's development, and for the story itself, is Mendel (which means "Comforter") Teichmann, a Jew who teaches the art of storytelling.

The new perspectives in *Jakob der Lügner* and *Der siebente Brunnen* result in part from a new narrative point of view. Apitz's narrator, for example, is omniscient and omnipresent, as is, it seems, his Party: "The Party with which they were intimately connected was with them in the camp: invisible, untouchable, omnipresent" (34). Apitz's final metaphor, a wave-like surge of humanity bursting the confines of Buchenwald, exudes confidence and optimism. Becker's and Wander's narrators, on the other hand, are single voices. These Jewish narrators know they have survived by accident. Lonely, melancholy, and sometimes bitter, removed from the easy answers of religious or political dogma, they grope with their writing toward tentative meaning.

Jurek Becker had originally conceived of *Jakob der Lügner* as a film, but the director of choice, Frank Beyer, fell into disfavor after a Party crackdown on artists and intellectuals in 1965. By the mid-1970s the cultural situation had changed, and Beyer collaborated with Becker on a sensitive, understated film version of the novel. Together with *Sterne*, it constitutes one of East Germany's most important cinematic responses to the Holocaust. The movie resonated internationally, receiving East Germany's first and only Oscar nomination for best foreign film. In the *New York Times Book Review*, Eva Figes later called it "for me the most moving film ever made on the harrowing topic of Europe's Jews during the last war" (27 Nov. 1988). Like Becker's novel, the film's emphasis on Jewish suffering, and its depiction of other forms of resistance, swerves from the instrumentalized East German antifascist discourse; but as Beyer insisted to me in conversation, that same discourse also generated both book and film.[25]

Issues of narration — the maintenance of humanity by story-telling; the necessity and impossibility of reporting the horror — are central to *Jakob der Lügner* and *Der siebente Brunnen* and are embodied in the figures of Jakob Heym and Mendel Teichmann. The former is in fact a modern-day Scheherazade, who kept death at bay by telling stories. In his third novel, *Der Boxer* (The Boxer, 1976), Jurek Becker continues to underscore the difficulties of bearing witness. His use of narration as a self-referential theme allows him to write one of the more ambiguous — and hence realistic — East German responses to the Holocaust.

The novel is set in the GDR in the late 1960s or early 1970s. The narrator, a sympathetic, somewhat naively orthodox East German man, has been interviewing Arno Blank, a survivor who, persecuted as a Jew, lost his wife and two children during the Second World War. After the war Blank stays in the GDR, changes his name from Aron to Arno, and with the help of the American Jewish aid organization Joint locates a boy, Mark, who may or may not be his son. Arno relates his family's story to the narrator, who writes it for us. Hence we have Arno's story — and his son's — through the well-meaning but limited refractory of the interlocutor. The narrator's occasional naiveté does not extend to his grasp of narrative theory; he knows that no experience can be replaced by its description, not even the best (238). He knows, too, that Arno often allows him only hints, combined with gestures or meaningful glances, so that he must interpret, extrapolate, and invent in order to fill the many gaps

(8–9). With clear echoes of Uwe Johnson's famous novel about the difficulty of reconstructing a life as a meaningful narrative, *Mutmaßungen über Jakob* (Speculations about Jakob, 1959), Becker's *Der Boxer* contains numerous references to "speculation," "hinting," and "interpreting." The narrator's search for meaning mirrors in a sense the reader's own; into the narrative gaps the reader projects his or her own meanings. The gaps also provide, incidentally or not, protection from the censor. Arno notes that he is telling a story (*erzählen*), not explaining (*erklären*); and if the narrator would often like to prove or document his own speculations, he knows he cannot (154). Hence key ideological questions, such as Arno's opinion of the GDR (249), or the reasons for Mark's eventual flight from that country, remain open. The narrator, the reader, Arno, and the censor can only speculate and provide their own interpretations.

The free space provided by the play of interpretations allows Becker to undertake some important revisions of East German Holocaust discourse, while at the same time remaining within the parameters of that master discourse. The relief organization Joint helps Arno find his lost son, and Paula, a Joint official, becomes Arno's first lover after the war. When Arno first kisses Paula, he asserts that he was in fact kissing Joint (36); one need only compare that with the East German condemnation of Paul Merker as a Zionist lackey and American spy in 1952: "[Merker] called on all comrades of Jewish descent to join the Jewish Community, *ostensibly*, so that they would have the pleasure of receiving Care packages from the American spy-central Joint, but in reality, so that the comrades would become beholden to that imperialist agency" ("Lehren" 208).

Becker's narrative techniques (as well as his own Jewish background and personal history) also allow him to explore tensions between Germans and Jewish-Germans. Arno maintains, if against his will, a rhetoric of us and them, and he views the narrator as an outsider. He perceives a school yard attack on Mark as a pogrom *in nuce*, and he fears the 17 June 1953 workers' uprising as the beginning of a pogrom. In this context he characterizes (East) Germany as "enemy territory" (256). Able to speak three languages, Arno can move between countries and cultures; resisting Cold War pressures for the neatness of dichotomous oppositions, he insists that he can see ten sides of an issue (208).

The story of Mark, who has no voice (except in one letter that the narrator reads) and is reconstructed by Arno and the narrator, also partakes of the ambiguity characterizing the novel. Mark can be made to figure Israel. The text often includes military language reminiscent of the Middle East when referring to him (e.g., *Vergeltungsaktion* [retaliatory action] 220, 239), and Mark, who learns boxing and may or may not misuse his power by abusing his schoolmates (here, as elsewhere, the text simultaneously demands and resists interpretation) can be made to illustrate the *"Aggressor-Staat-Israel"* of East German propaganda. But that is only one interpretation. That Mark reads the Bible; that he is close to the camp survivor Kenick, a Zionist who emigrates to Palestine in the 1940s; that he chooses mathematics as a field of study in order to avoid political interference; that he flees to the West; that he emigrates to Israel and quite possibly dies fighting for the Israelis in the 1967 war: all this contributes to a negative figure by official East German standards but not necessarily for other readers (including those in the GDR). And as the son of the central figure Arno,[26] for whom we develop some degree of sympathy, Mark inevitably claims some of that sympathy as well. Furthermore, as Sander Gilman has pointed out, Mark shares autobiographical traits with Becker and serves as a kind of alter ego for the author.[27] Again, the resulting tensions open the text.

Perhaps more important, *Der Boxer* demonstrates that the "Jewish question" was not solved by the East German rhetoric of assimilation into the melting pot of socialism, to speak with Zweig. Arno Blank, with his ruined life, is no example of the positive hero, of the *Aufbau* pathos, or of the "Victors of History" — all tropes with which the East Germans attempted to define themselves. *Der Boxer* is furthermore a landmark in Becker's long preoccupation with what it means to be Jewish. "Am I Jewish?" Arno asks the narrator who, uncertain, dismisses the question as an attempt at humor (251). And although the narrator consistently calls Arno by his Jewish name Aron, he appears perplexed when he notices that Arno often speaks as though he were being assigned against his will to a group (255). Arno makes this point more specific near the conclusion of the novel. The narrator recalls the conversation:

[Aron] asked me what in the world Jewishness was besides a religious decision. Didn't we finally live in a time, he asked, in which everyone could decide for himself alone to which political party he wished to belong? He had no influence of course as to whether he was Turkish or German, but did that apply to Christianity and Judaism? A child of Catholic parents could freely decide when he came of age whether or not to be Catholic. Why, he asked me, did one deny the children of Jewish parents the same right? (298)

Precisely this question recurs in Becker's novel *Bronsteins Kinder* (Bronstein's Children, 1986).[28] The novel takes place in the GDR in the early 1970s, at about the time *Der Boxer* concluded. It is narrated by Hans Bronstein, the teenage son of a Jewish concentration camp survivor named Arno. Hans discovers that his father and two other survivors have kidnapped a former concentration camp guard and are holding him under degrading conditions in a secluded summer cottage. The identical names of the fathers in *The Boxer* and *Bronsteins Kinder* indicate the most obvious of many thematic similarities and intertextual references between the two novels. Formally the two texts resemble each other in that they are told by narrators who can only guess at the thoughts, feelings, and motivations of the two fathers (in the case of *Bronsteins Kinder*, the son Hans narrates the story after his father's death), hence creating an "open" narrative.

Although Hans considers his father "normal"[29] and "wonderfully intact" (219), he admits "that, in dealing with people over fifty, Father tended to be unjust and rude" (47). Arno's accomplice, Gordon Kwart, insists that East German Jews continue to reside in "hostile territory" (161), and Hans remembers one conversation with his father and his father's accomplices, during which the older Jews "agreed they were living in an inferior country, surrounded by second-rate people who didn't deserve any better" (296). For Arno Bronstein, the antifascist program of the Democratic Republic is an accident, a formality, a facade: there are no good Germans.

Having been socialized in East Germany, Hans has not thought about Jewish issues (66), and he generally engages in a massive act of repression, a project his girlfriend exposes:

> I've known for a long time that there is a certain subject one cannot discuss with you . . . . The moment there's a word starting with J, you break out in a sweat. The real victims are forever wanting to celebrate memorial days and organize vigils, and you want silence to be kept. Maybe you imagine that to be the opposite, but let me tell you: it's the same hang-up. (219)

Hans admits only once, tentatively, that the past may have damaged his present: "Perhaps I am a victim of Fascism after all and refuse to admit it" (194). He will not utilize the official designation "victim of fascism" to secure himself a scarce apartment (176), but he does include himself in that category to facilitate his acceptance at the university (5).

That ambivalence governs many of Hans's thoughts and actions. Although a firm believer in assimilation, he has a Jewish girlfriend (at that time there were perhaps 400 Jews in East Berlin, a city of over a million people) (O'Doherty 244). During several key exchanges in the novel, he wonders whether non-Jewish members of his society regard him as a Jew (see, for example, 37 or 171); through skillful use of ambiguity, Becker leaves the question open. Hans's Jewish relatives and acquaintances clearly consider Hans Jewish: their rhetoric is of "us" and "our people." Hans is less certain. The novel works extensively with images of heredity, role-playing, and socialization, presenting, like *Der Boxer*, an extended musing on Sartre's dictum that the Jew is one whom others consider a Jew.[30]

Originally entitling his novel *How I Became a German*, Becker ultimately called it *Bronstein's Children*. The title thus emphasizes not the optimistic (East) German project of enlightenment and assimilation, but rather the ties of generations and history. The novel continues the revisionist project pursued by some East German writers since the 1970s, that concerned with exposing the East German myth of an abrupt, revolutionary rupture with the negative traditions of German history. Becker instead investigates continuities, at least from the viewpoint of the victims and their offspring. Hans generally considers himself to be neither Jewish nor a victim of fascism, but the text demonstrates that in crucial ways he is both.

The novel contains several standard topoi of East German literature. Becker has noted, for example, that he sees it as a criticism of Israeli actions (Hage 337). In another typical East German gesture, Hans repeatedly compares West Germany unfavorably with his country, and at the conclusion the former camp guard flees West. An antifascist film mentioned in the story recalls the traditional East German emphasis on Communist resistance. While reading the script Hans muses:

> The story was about a Resistance group, of which one member was a Jewish girl — Rahel. All the members lived with false documents

and were in the same danger. Consequently it made no difference to Rahel that she was Jewish — at least that's how I took it. (92)

Becker ironizes here the East German equation of Jews and Communists as equivalent victims of fascism. Implicit is also the questioning of a view common to many Jews on the left that the melting pot of Communism "offset" their Jewishness. As Hans Mayer wrote: "Trotsky always dismissed his Judaism — and not without elements of self-hatred — as an accident of birth. His life history disproved this thesis" (Schultz 257). Mayer then outlines Stalin's anti-Semitic purges and trials. Trotsky's original surname was Bronstein. By raising the specificity of the "Jewish question," Becker interrogates official and literary versions of Zweig's melting pot or Hermlin's "time together," either during the Second World War or in the GDR.

Bronsteins Kinder was written and published by Becker after he left the GDR. Living in West Berlin with dual citizenship, the author possessed considerably more artistic and intellectual freedom than in East Germany. But the novel did appear in the GDR in 1987, a year after its publication in the West. On its surface, at any rate, Becker's text fits easily into the state-inspired renaissance of Jewish topics during the final days of East Germany, while adhering to the state-sponsored discourse that privileged assimilation and criticism of Israel.

In the years between 1945–1990, the cultural production in the Soviet Occupation Zone and the GDR grew increasingly sophisticated in its treatment of anti-Semitism and, with that, its response to the Holocaust and its symbolic construction of Judaism. We can trace some of these changes in the writing of Stefan Heym.

Born in 1913 in Chemnitz, Germany, to a family of practicing Jews, Heym early became involved in left-wing activities. Doubly endangered, he fled Germany in 1933. Heym took refuge in Czechoslovakia and then the United States, where he had success as a novelist. Somewhat like the young Konrad Wolf, who invaded his native Germany with the Red Army, Heym was drafted by the US army and fought against the Nazis as a member of a psychological warfare unit in Germany. After the war his pro-Communist sentiments led to increasing friction with his adopted country; his novels regularly compare the treatment of American leftists with the Nazi persecution of the Jews. During the Korean War Heym left the United States, taking asylum first in Communist Czechoslovakia, then in East Germany.

In Heym's first East German novel, *Die Papiere des Andreas Lenz* (The Lenz Papers, 1963), the Jewish capitalist Einstein insists that Germany needs a customs union and railroads more than the freedom and democracy espoused by the 1848 revolutionaries in Baden:

> For me, personalities, political philosophy, and methods of government are not important as long as the foundation is laid for the requirements of our financial and economic system. The question as to who lays that foundation interests me less than the dirt under my fingernails — as long as it occurs. And I'm ready to pay what is necessary . . . . (460)

To achieve his ends, Einstein will work with anyone, even the democrats, though their fizzled revolution has convinced him that the democratic cause is hardly efficacious. He suspects that the only way to create the financial opportunities he envisions will be through a police state (604). Among other things, Heym wants the reader to think of German fascism, of the Marxist commonplace (since the Comintern) that fascism represents the final, most radical and aggressive stage of capitalism, and that German finance capital carried Hitler to power. Heym, a man of Jewish descent, is here blaming "Jewish" finance. He tries to balance his portrayal of Einstein with another stereotype, that of the Jewish revolutionary, in this case Einstein's beautiful daughter Leonore.

Heym's novel *Lassalle*, a biographical novel concerning the eponymous nineteenth-century German-Jewish socialist leader, appeared in West Germany in 1969 but only in a limited East German edition in 1974, during a brief cultural liberalization. Heym's portrayal of Lassalle, a contemporary and rival of Marx, is ultimately negative, but it is not unambiguous, and as Paul O'Doherty points out, Lassalle's life and actions should be seen as a response to the deeply ingrained anti-Semitism of his society (*Portrayal* 170–78). Much of that anti-Semitism can be located within the structures of the conservative Prussian establishment, but Heym also appends correspondence between Marx and Engels in which they discuss Lassalle using anti-Semitic slurs. Heym thus places Lassalle's life within the context of a web of anti-Semitism from the left and the right.

Left-wing anti-Semitism was and remained an explosive issue in the GDR, as demonstrated in part by the suppression of Heym's novel *Collin* (1979). The book, which could only appear in the West, violated numerous taboos; most importantly for our purposes, Heym includes the story of Paul Merker, the Communist official who, in the 1950s, was imprisoned in large part due to his advocacy of paying reparations to Jews. In *Collin* Heym portrays Paul Merker as Paul Faber, a Party official who, though innocent, is arrested as a Zionist agent and imprisoned under degrading conditions. The crime against Faber forms one cause of the disease that, years later, afflicts the writer Collin and Urack, the head of State Security. The illness hobbling these two men stands in synecdochical relation to the unexpiated past that cripples East Germany.

In *Ahasver* (The Wandering Jew, 1981), Heym satirizes the East Germans' preparation of a Luther-Year for 1983, emphasizing not only Luther's condemnation of the peasants' revolt but also his anti-Semitism. The Israeli professor (and "devil") Leuchtentrager correctly reminds the East German professor Beifuß that Luther, whom the GDR wishes to honor, published vehemently anti-Jewish tracts, and that later anti-Semites, including the Nazis, utilized Lutheran slogans.

As East German artists acknowledged the tenacity of anti-Semitism (also within socialism), they began to display more sympathy for Israel. In *Ahasver*, Heym attacks official policy by satirizing East Germany's relationship, or lack thereof, with that country. Beifuß encounters difficulties with State Security due to his correspondence with Leuchtentrager, since the government expects support for the Party line, even if that entails a *sacrifizio d'intelletto*. A government official writes:

> I would suggest your giving some thought to the preparation of a project through which . . . you might prove the close interaction of religion and imperialist expansionism, particularly in relation to Israel. I am stressing Israel because we observe similar tendencies in Islamic countries as well; these, however, we will disregard in view of the political aims pursued by our Soviet friends and ourselves.
>
> (*The Wandering* 94)

Heym thus emphasizes the one-sided presentation in East Germany of the Arab-Israeli conflict. But his novel could not appear in the GDR until 1988.

Heym's novel *Schwarzenberg* (1984) unfolds in Germany at the conclusion of the Second World War. In this novel Max Wolfram returns to his native village and learns how his father, a Jew, had had his belongings confiscated, his hair shorn, and had been exposed to public ridicule while his wife carted him around the market place in a wheelbarrow. The narrator, a German Communist, asks himself:

> Why do I concern myself so with [Max]? I was not beholden to him in any way, nor to his father, who to be sure ultimately committed suicide, but to whom I had been bound neither by friendship nor by other relationships. In fact, with my pigeonhole thinking I had always counted him as part of the class of exploiters until I saw him sitting half-dazed in that wheelbarrow. (22)

In this brief passage, we encounter Heym's realization that a mechanical theoretical construct of class will not suffice to explain all aspects of anti-Semitism, and that to the extent that Marxists equate Jews and capitalists (or, for that matter, Jews and revolutionaries), their own vision may be clouded by anti-Semitic prejudice. These sentences from *Schwarzenberg* (a novel which first appeared in the GDR after the Wall opened) read as a corrective, twenty-one years later, to those in *Die Papiere des Andreas Lenz*.

Finally, in a speech delivered in West Germany in 1988, Heym outlines — as he did in *Ahasver* — some of the economic foundations for anti-Semitism, only ultimately to reject that line of thought when discussing contemporary anti-Semitism in West and, more surprisingly, East Germany. Referring to organized right-wing activity among East German youth, Heym correctly points out that, according to Marxist theory, such things were simply impossible ("Schreiben" 231–33). And in fact his government publicly ignored such activities or, when forced to take cognizance of them, dismissed them as West German imports.

In the 1970s East German writers began haltingly to interrogate the Stalinist as well as the Nazi past and, as we saw with Stefan Heym's *Lassalle* and *Collin*, this included the situation of Jews in Communist parties or countries. Like Arnold Zweig, Carl Jakob Danzinger (Joachim Chaim Schwarz) became disillusioned with Palestine during his exile there, and he came to the GDR a convinced Marxist. The SED, however, considered him a Zionist. In his autobiographical novel, *Die Partei hat immer recht* (The Party Is Always Right, 1976), Danzinger describes the difficulties he and other Jews encountered in the GDR during the 1950s. Danzinger's writing continues the project of revising earlier Marxist positions. Like Stephan Hermlin in *Die erste Reihe* for example, Danzinger discusses the Herbert Baum resistance group, but whereas in the 1950s Hermlin had celebrated its members as Jewish-Communist antifascists (with the emphasis on their Communism), Danzinger questions "what value their assimilation was; why they created this special group and were not assimilated into the illegal Communist Party. Was there something in this world that could not be explained according to Marxist categories?" (237). Such questions lead Danzinger, near the conclusion of his text (published only in the West) to a strong declaration of sympathy for Israel.

The narrator of Stephan Hermlin's autobiographical *Abendlicht* (Evening Light, 1979) writes:

> In Lenin I had read that even the slightest trace of anti-Semitism is evidence of the reactionary character of the group or individual that exhibits it. I could see this remark contained a kind of formula, a quasi-mathematical equation. Wherever the cowardly pestilence raised its head, there could be no socialism, all noble words to the contrary. (*Evening Light* 94)

In the context of the novel, this passage refers to National Socialism. It contains a subtext, however, which we can decipher by referring to a 1979 interview, cited in Chapter 3, between Hermlin and his West German publisher. During the interview Hermlin noted: "The Jewish question, which for a number of years was repressed in our country due to the influence of certain developments in other socialist countries — let us say repressed, anything else would be unjust to the GDR, which up to now has behaved honorably in this matter — this Jewish question is today being openly discussed" (Hermlin, "Wo" 400). In an interview that Hermlin held in 1983 with East German scholar Silvia Schlenstedt, an interview that in many ways reads as a gloss on *Abendlicht*, he registers his abhorrence of anti-Semitism and adds in this regard that "certain occurrences in socialist countries have made not only me uneasy, they are an occasion for disquiet for every single Socialist or Communist" (Schlenstedt, *Hermlin* 22).

Günter Kunert's 1978 essay "Oranienburger Strasse 28," (Site of the Berlin Jewish Community's library that was reopened in the mid-1970s) compares the narrator with an archeologist (208) examining relicts "which are not bound to their own origin by tradition, remembrance, or any other kind of interest in conservation"

(210). With a tone that moves between anger and mourning, the narrator (in many ways a Kunert self-portrait) remembers his family, including his Jewish grandparents who were murdered at Auschwitz. The essay includes bitter sideswipes at East German planners who let Jewish monuments rot (207); it hints at nascent anti-Semitism (207); it repeatedly regrets the absence of Jewish history in East Germany; and it mentions the absence of the Archives of German Jewry (*Gesamtarchiv der deutschen Juden*), confiscated first by the Nazis, then by the East German government.[31] For Kunert, German Jews are figured by the presence of absence, an absence that furthermore does not appear particularly to trouble his contemporaries. In *Memento* (1966), a restrained documentary film for which Kunert helped write the script, the author had utilized a similar approach. The film examines Jewish graveyards (including their neglect)[32] in the GDR, and the film twice speaks of "the forgotten memory of those who lived. The cries of the murdered whisper in the wind to which no one listens."[33]

In *Herr Moses in Berlin* (1979) Heinz Knobloch employs, like Kunert, what he terms an "archeological methodology" (15) to describe the excavation of a buried past (and we recall that Hermlin, too, spoke of a past that had been repressed). *Herr Moses in Berlin* excavates the life of the eighteenth-century philosopher Moses Mendelssohn, but it also describes the vicissitudes of Jews in Communism. Knobloch notes: "Inexorably, the current day makes itself noticeable during the writing process, and it should" (17). Like Christa Wolf in *Kindheitsmuster* (Patterns of Childhood, 1976), Knobloch moves among various historical moments in order to underscore sometimes troubling continuities.

Knobloch's examination of anti-Semitism from the 1700s to the present stresses questions of class and economics, but he ventures beyond that. He quotes, for example, an East German youth encyclopedia that reproduces the Party line: Jews are persecuted because the ruling exploitative classes wish to distract attention from economic exploitation and oppression, the true causes of misery. Knobloch contradicts that definition, noting that not only "exploitative classes" have persecuted Jews. Like Hermlin in *Abendlicht*, he cites a speech by Lenin in which the Soviet leader condemns anti-Semitism as reactionary ignorance. Knobloch then inserts a laconic remark from a fictional Comrade Cohn: "It appears they didn't all hear this [speech]" (80). Twelve pages later Knobloch abruptly volunteers the following information:

> Mosche Kulbalk. Born in 1896 in Smorgon, near Vilnia. Father a forester. Studied at a Talmud school and wrote his first poems in Hebrew. 1920 in Berlin. 1923 teacher for literature at the Jewish High School in Vilnia. Authored works in poetry, prose, and drama. As of 1928 in the Soviet Union. Arrested in 1937 under false pretenses. Died in a camp in 1940. Later rehabilitated. (92)

With his pointed reference to a Soviet Jewish writer who died in the Gulag, Knobloch documents his assertion that Jews have not been persecuted by "exploitative classes" alone. He understands the scapegoat psychology informing much anti-Semitism, and knows that such psychology is not limited by economic system.

"Marina Roza" (1986), a story published in the West by Barbara Honigmann, also addresses the situation of Soviet Jews. The story tells of a visit to Soviet Hasidic Jews who are harassed and spied upon by their government. In 1982 the government disbands the synagogue, arrests the Jews, and sends some to Siberia. The East German narrator and her husband never hear from them again. During a 1986 interview, author Honigmann described her own background, noting that her parents, of Jewish descent, returned to Germany in 1947 from exile in England. They raised their daughter as a Communist and an atheist; nonetheless, she developed a Jewish identity (a not unusual development, as we have seen in Chapter 3) and left the GDR in 1984 for Strasbourg, the "Jerusalem of the West" (Thomalla).

In Jan Koplowitz's story "Karfunkel und der Taschendieb" (Karfunkel and the Pickpocket, 1988) the Communist Karfunkel, of Jewish descent, describes his successful postwar career in Poland: "Until my Polish Workers' Party was stung by the malaria mosquito of anti-Semitism." (61). Karfunkel falls victim to political purges but is not physically harmed. He claims that matters have righted themselves, though "many Jewish comrades have left Poland or have had to leave Poland" (61).

Stefan Heym's autobiography, *Nachruf* (Obituary, 1988), contains numerous allusions to the treatment of Jews in other Communist countries, for example the Soviet "doctors' plot."[34] Heym, who sought asylum in Czechoslovakia during the early 1950s, makes repeated reference to Czech Central Committee member Rudolf Slánský, sentenced during an anti-Semitic Stalinist

show trial. Heym surmised that had he remained in Czechoslovakia, he — a former American intelligence officer of Jewish descent — might have been arrested as well (529). *Nachruf* was not
published in East Germany. Heym's post-unification novel *Radek*
deals with the Polish-Jewish revolutionary Karl Radek, who becomes a victim of Stalin's show trials and is subsequently murdered in the Gulag.

Elsewhere in this study we have noted that the 1980s, and especially
the period after 1985, brought greater flexibility and openness for
East German citizens responding to the Holocaust. The reasons for
this are varied, but they include state interest (the continuing need
to profile East Germany against West Germany, or the growing desire to achieve better economic relations with the United States) and
an incipient *glasnost*. As the former East German Elke Schieber
points out, however, there were other reasons as well: "The 1980s
demonstrate changes in West and East Germany regarding the attitude of Germans toward their crimes against the Jews in Germany
and in Europe. Perhaps decades had to pass before the shame was
overcome to the extent that one could raise one's eyes and look at
the horror" (228). These new attitudes compete with the old ones
in many of the not inconsiderable number of Holocaust films,
mostly documentary, that were released in the GDR during the
1980s.

    In 1980, after West German Chancellor Helmut Kohl had de-
manded (in vain) that the East Germans air the US television melodrama *Holocaust*, the GDR released the documentary film *Dawids
Tagebuch* (Dawid's Diary) based on the writing of the twelve-year-
old Polish Jew Dawid Rubinowicz. Dawid's diary, which breaks off
in mid-sentence, records the increasing pressure and degradation to
which he and the other Jews in his village were subjected between
1939–42. In 1942 he was deported to Auschwitz and murdered.
The film's narrative culminates with the assertion that "children were
the youngest resistance fighters," an indication that Dawid's defiant
detailing of events could now be incorporated into an expanding
East German lexicon of resistance.

    As preparation for the state-sponsored commemoration of the
1938 November pogrom, DEFA released several films. The docu-

mentary *Moses Mendelssohn: Ein Weltweiser aus Berlin* (Moses Mendelssohn: A Wise Berliner Who Showed the Way into the World) of 1985 concludes with a reference to the 1945 Berlin production of Lessing's *Nathan der Weise,* for which the assimilationist Mendelssohn had served as model for the enlightened Nathan. Roza Berger-Fiedler's *Erinnern heißt leben* (To Remember Means to Live, 1987) pieces together, like Knobloch's Mendelssohn book or the documentary film on the same subject, German-Jewish relations through a mosaic of gravestones. Her subjective, first-person narrative traces German national history through the history of her own family. The documentary *Die Lüge und der Tod* (The Lie and Death, 1988) uses footage filmed by the Nazis in 1941 to document their efficiency in preparing Jews for deportation. The text was written and spoken by writer Stephan Hermlin. By turns subtle, ironic, silent, and indignant, Hermlin infuses the short film with considerable power. *Jeder konnte es sehen* (Everyone Could See It, 1988) begins with an act of (non-Communist) Jewish resistance: Herschel Grynszpan's shooting of a Nazi diplomat after the deportation of thousands of Polish Jews, among them Grynszpan's family, from Germany. The film contains some standard East German elements: a muted reference to Globke, no reference to the Hitler-Stalin pact, and final, strongly associative scenes that feature advertisements from 4711 Eau de Cologne and Volkswagen supporting the Nazis in 1938. But it contains more unusual elements as well, for example the text that provides the emotional and logical climax:

> By watching and keeping quiet the German people began to be guilty. There was shame and courage. Humanity and dignity and solidarity. People that helped. From all classes. There were few of them. Too few.

Also in 1988 DEFA released the feature film *Die Schauspielerin* (The Actress), based on a work by author Hedda Zinner. Set in Nazi Germany, the film narrates the story of a young, gentile actress, "the incarnation of Germanism" and "the ideal German woman," who at the height of her success in Munich feigns suicide, changes her identity to that of a Jew, and joins her Jewish lover in Berlin. Under increasingly restrictive conditions they work for the Jewish theater and await their fate. The film echoes aspects of the plays *Der Stellvertreter* by West German playwright Rolf Hochhuth, and *Andorra* (1961) by Swiss author Max Frisch, but most clearly for an East German audience it cites the early DEFA classic *Ehe im Schatten,* especially with its formal devices and shots of mirrors, stages, and windows, shots that emphasize the gaze. Elements of the standard East German discourse can be glimpsed in the film's imbrication of blacks, Communists, and Jews, but it does not belabor these points.[35] Martin Brandt, the sole survivor of the Berlin Jewish theater and the subject of a DEFA documentary from 1989, plays a small role.

These new accents and possibilities emerged from a conflicted cultural landscape in which previously suppressed voices began to emerge but continued to jostle, overlap, and compete with more orthodox discourse. In 1978 the attempt by DEFA to film *Damit die Nacht nicht wiederkehre* (That the Night Does Not Return), based on the autobiography of the East German Rabbi Martin Riesenburger, was abruptly halted after the first day of filming. (Eastern German film historian Elke Schieber suspects an intervention from Moscow) (228). Peter Rocha's television film *Sonst wären wir verloren* (Otherwise We Would Be Lost, 1981) planned to have the famous Buchenwald child, Stefan Zerzy Zweig, as its focus. Because Zweig had since left the GDR, the state hindered Rocha (according to the latter) in numerous ways. Although Rocha succeeded in contacting Zweig and in shooting numerous scenes with him, little of that footage ultimately made its way into his finished film (Schieber 230). *Das Jahr 1945* (The Year 1945), one of the most important and widely viewed DEFA documentary films of the 1980s, does not mention the persecution and murder of 6 million Jews. When viewers called this to the attention of directors Karl Gass and Klaus Wischnewski, Gass noted: "We were very shocked. We were simply not conscious of having omitted that" (cited in Schieber 230). *Das Singen im Dom zu Magdeburg* (Singing in the Magdeburg Cathedral, 1986) depicts West Berlin cantor Estrongo Nachama, an Auschwitz survivor, singing with a Christian choir in the East German Magdeburg Cathedral; at the time of the filming, cantor and choir had collaborated for eight years. Although the film is explicit about the murder of Magdeburg's Jews, it nonetheless emphasizes the suffering and death of Magdeburg's non-Jewish citizens during Allied bombardments. In its very structure, the film establishes two opposing sets of victims, but it shows no awareness of how problematical its undertaking is. Roza Berger-Fiedler's important *Erinnern heißt leben* had no state funding, and even in the more supportive atmosphere of the later 1980s the director had difficulty screening it;

critics dismissed the documentary as being unsuccessful in both form and content (Schieber 231). *Der Mann an der Rampe* (The Man at the Ramp), of 1989, features familiar attacks against the Federal Republic as a haven for Nazis.

The films of the 1980s were made to reinforce the Party line and/or educate about the past. Either way, as demonstrated for example by the documentary on Moses Mendelssohn, the overriding message remained that of dialogue and assimilation. Only rarely, such as in the reactions to the premier of Peter Rocha's *Das Singen im Dom zu Magdeburg,* could and did East German audiences articulate those "suppressed feelings and thoughts" which, as Elke Schieber asserts, "were not discussed in the public sphere": the possibility that, after Auschwitz, there could be no Christian-Jewish dialogue (231).

East German artists of Jewish descent dealt with "Jewish" themes in a variety of ways. Some, like Anna Seghers or Wolf Biermann, avoided such themes almost completely.[36] Others, like the artist and Auschwitz survivor Peter Edel, adhered closely to the master discourse. Still others, as I have demonstrated in this chapter, interrogated orthodox interpretations either openly or between the lines. Regardless of the intentions of the creator, the workings of the artistic medium at times open unexpected aporias that reveal moments of vulnerability, residues of otherness, the insider as outsider.

The frame narrator of Hermlin's "Die Zeit der Gemeinsamkeit," who visits the ruins of the Warsaw Ghetto after the war, is in a sense doubly displaced: as a German and, presumably, as a Jew. Jonathan Ross has rightly pointed out that the narrator attempts to identify with the new socialist state, but nonetheless feels not quite at one with it. At the same time the narrator is drawn to the ruins; his visit, the text several times notes, has a clandestine quality (Ross 262–65). It is, the narrator muses, as if he were following secret orders and attending a secret meeting.

Gertrud Koch sees in the films of Konrad Wolf a process of vanishing, forgetting, and repressing:

> [W]e can imagine all of the profound adjustments which this young man had to make: the son of German-Jewish emigrants, who, in Soviet uniform, was involved in the liberation of the concentration

camp Sachsenhausen at the age of nineteen, then became a twenty-year-old film student back in Moscow, where he had spent his childhood and youth, only to experience there, or perhaps also to overlook or to repress, the way in which the cold war propaganda was making use of anti-Semitic stereotypes. It then becomes somewhat clearer why, in the films of Konrad Wolf, the subject of Jewish annihilation remains ever present although in its own peculiar way; why, at the same time, he addresses the subject and goes on from there in accordance with the ideological party line. Yet in doing so and precisely by thematizing it, the films display more of the tensions which lie in the confusions of identity between Berlin, Moscow, and the imaginary Jerusalem . . . . (62)

In *Professor Mamlock*, for example, the protagonist is "starkly schematic," but "traces of subjectivity" can be glimpsed in an episode where his Jewish daughter is stigmatized at school (Koch 70). *Ich war neunzehn* (I Was Nineteen, 1968) features the liberation of Sachsenhausen but nowhere mentions that in addition to Eastern Europeans, Jews were also murdered there. Yet through his images Wolf built in a "latent self-identification with the Jews who were gassed" (Koch 73). Cut into the staged Soviet documentary film *The Hangman of Sachsenhausen*, which Wolf includes in *Ich war neunzehn*, he also adds a parallel montage of the protagonist under a shower, frozen in fear. No one identity in the confusing mix of German-Jew, Soviet soldier, and German Communist can provide protection. Konrad Wolf's films present in such moments the "images of being a foreigner in one's home" (Koch 75). One senses a different but related moment of vulnerability in Stefan Heym's autobiography, when, soon after having fled the United States for the East bloc, he hears of the Soviet "doctors' trial": "And then the names came, which sounded noticeably Jewish" (*Nachruf* 563).

Alterity, real and imagined, represents a recurring topic in the works of Jurek Becker. Sander Gilman points out that *Jakob der Lügner* revises the stereotype of the lying Jew; *Der Boxer* the stereotype of the silent Jew; and *Bronsteins Kinder* that of the secret language of the Jews ("Jüdische" 278–86). Becker continually thematizes the difficulties between Jewish-Germans and Germans. In *Jakob der Lügner* the postwar narrator despairs of making his story known to non-Jewish Germans: "I've tried hundreds of times to unload this blasted story, without success. Either I tried it with the wrong people, or I made some mistake or the other. I mixed up a lot of things, I got names wrong or, as I said, they were the wrong people" (*Jakob the Liar* 8). In *Der Boxer* Arno's history inhibits communication between him and other Germans, and against his will, he raises his son to be an outsider, a paradigm repeated in *Bronsteins Kinder*. The Jews in both novels continue to speak of East Germany as enemy territory.

In "Rohstoff, unsichtbar" Günter Kunert describes the failure of his assimilated parents to reconstitute the Weimar Republic in the GDR, a failure in part due to the Holocaust and the resulting absence of those who had formerly been a part of the Weimar experiment (251). One felt oneself ever more the melancholy Other (*fremd*); his contemporaries pitied him, he writes, like one would a handicapped person who also lives on the edge of society (251). That sense of melancholy and alterity also shimmers through Kunert's "Oranienburger Straße 28," where the narrator finds traces of himself, his parents, and other family members in crumbling Nazi files within the shabby headquarters of the clearly neglected, clearly irrelevant East Berlin Jewish Community.

Can we draw general conclusions from this myriad of examples? To begin with, East German literature and film essayed — generally in a philosemitic manner — to reintroduce Jews as human beings to a German public. Two years after the end of the Second World War, the film *Ehe im Schatten* utilizes the rather daring technique of allowing the German audience to identify with a protagonist who only later is revealed to be Jewish. And more so than in West Germany, East German artists confronted the Holocaust, although they did so within the parameters of a state-supporting antifascist discourse. This chapter has demonstrated the fashion in which writers and filmmakers helped construct that discourse.

With occasional exceptions, East German cultural production portrayed German Jewishness as something from the past, and Jewish religion as negative. According to East German Holocaust discourse, Jews in the Third Reich, blinded by religion or their class standpoint (Jews are often portrayed as capitalists), failed to perceive the danger represented by the Nazis and hence must carry some of the blame for their own deaths. (That charge appeared in the infamous SED pamphlet attacking Slánský and Paul Merker, and it remained a constant in East German Holocaust discourse ["Lehren"

207]). Contemporary Jews appeared primarily within East German works designed to condemn resurgent anti-Semitism in West Germany or fascist tendencies in Israel.

More generally, East German culture depicted Jews as victims, especially though not exclusively as victims of the Nazis. Jews constituted one group of victims among many, but they provided a convenient shorthand to demonstrate and condemn the inhumanity of (capitalist) German fascism and to celebrate the heroism of the Communist opposition. East German writers and filmmakers not infrequently figured Jews as women (for example, *Ehe im Schatten, Sterne, Ravensbrücker Ballade*) or as children (for instance, "Das schweigende Dorf," *Nackt unter Wölfen, Der Regenwettermann, Geschichte von Moischele, Dawids Tagebuch*).[37] But in a sense the male figures are also gendered female, for they are generally passive, often naive, and almost always in need of aid, generally from Communists who advise, protect, defend, or liberate. Jeffrey Herf's general dictum applies particularly to cultural discourse in the GDR: "The old anti-Semitic stereotypes of the Jew as capitalist and as passive weakling would continue to lurk within the muscular Communist discourse of East German antifascism" (*Divided* 83). There are to be sure active, "masculine," Jewish-Communists — we see them for example in works by Peter Edel, Stephan Hermlin, Jan Koplowitz, and Konrad Wolf — but to a real extent these men have ceased to be Jews. (Just as the monument to Herbert Baum across from the East German Parliament elided his Jewishness). Two East German films depict postwar Jews carrying out acts of revenge, but those films are set in *West* Germany. *Bronsteins Kinder*, a literary work that treats a similar subject but which is set in East Germany (though the author had left that country), condemns the actions of the Jewish father.

Homi Bhabha has argued that culture is not something seamless and whole; artists undertake "performative interventions" that reveal culture not as made, but as being made. Even as East German cultural products helped to generate an instrumentalized, state-supporting Holocaust discourse, they could simultaneously if sometimes unwittingly reveal the aporias of that discourse. Indeed, as the years passed, East German artists interrogated with ever more insistence (though always incompletely) Marxist Holocaust discourse, and they began to question a theory of anti-Semitism that exclusively privileged economics. An attentive public could then ask, along with Carl Jakob Danzinger, whether there was indeed something in the world that could not be explained by the meta-narrative of Marx-ism.[38]

Several of the works I have discussed are archeological, in Knobloch's or Kunert's sense: they attempt to excavate the repressed past of which Hermlin and others spoke. And when Danzinger, Knobloch, Hermlin, Heym, B. Honigmann, Koplowitz, or Kunert address the difficulties of Jews in socialism, they necessarily modify the orthodox Marxist tenet that capitalists encourage anti-Semitism to displace the energies engendered by class struggle. Instead, they move closer to the idea, suggested by the later, more revisionist Horkheimer and Adorno, that rulers *in general* can profit from anti-Semitism. Implicitly and sometimes explicitly, they also queried the efficacy as well as the motives of East Germany's Enlightenment-grounded ideal of assimilation. In this they ventured considerably further than the historians of the former German Democratic Republic.

Notes

[1] For an exception, see Lauckner.

[2] Regarding the question of East German anti-Semitism, I in general agree with Herf: "The East German government was not an anti-Semitic regime in the sense that the Nazi regime was. Hatred for the Jewish people was not one of its core principles. But then neither did it display the kind of warmth or empathy that might be expected from any German government after the Holocaust. This conflict between antifascist legitimation and anti-Jewish policy constitutes a major, if too rarely noted, theme of East German history. The East Germans were willing to adopt the language of traditional European anti-Semitism. That cold-hearted willingness was apparent in the conspiracy accusations during the anticosmopolitan purges, and in the refusal to give adequate recognition to the memory of the Holocaust, to pay financial restitution to Jewish survivors, to conduct an adequate program of trials for crimes of the Nazi era in the 1950s, or to refrain from active partisanship on behalf of Israel's armed adversaries in the Middle East. The anticosmopolitan purge of winter 1952–53, the arrest and imprisonment of Paul Merker, the purging of those Jews and their sympathizers who supported restitution or opposed East Germany's active antagonism toward Israel, the flight of Leo Zuckermann and the leadership of the tiny Jewish community all irrevocably broke those bonds of solidarity which had emerged between some Communists and some Jews during the war. Those Jews who remained in the East German regime did so on terms of assimilation far more self-effacing than those accepted by German Jews before 1933." (*Divided* 384–85).

[3] A truly comprehensive survey would include biographies, children's literature, and perhaps literature in translation. Additionally, there are films I have been unable to view.

[4] *Professor Mamlock* 61. There is an echo of Wolf's Mamlock in Johannes R. Becher's play *Der Weg nach Füssen* (The Road to Füssen, 1956), where the Jewish capitalist Rosenzweig admits that his money had actually helped the Nazis attain power (54). See also Peter Edel's novel *Die Bilder des Zeugen Schattmann* (The Pictures of Witness Schattmann), in which a Jewish doctor — again, a Mamlock figure — blames his class for bringing to power those who will now destroy his "race" (166).

[5] On a basic level, one could find these same elements in an idealized sketch in the Sachsenhausen Jewish museum. The sketch depicted a heroic proletarian couple shielding a frightened Jewish doctor.

[6] The film's imagery makes frequent use of doors. By shutting them, Mamlock closes down communication between the Communists and himself.

[7] See, for example, pages 154–55 and 166.

[8] In 1981 a television film entitled "Hotel Polan und seine Gäste" was made of this novel. Koplowitz claims that he was removed from the project and that his dismissal provides evidence of anti-Semitism in the GDR. (O'Doherty, *Portrayal* 257–58). It is hard to understand why Koplowitz would have been removed from the film project, since the book hews closely to the Party line and explicitly rejects Zionism. Nonetheless, the project was highly controversial; Thomas Jung writes that the production process lasted 9 years, was repeatedly interrupted, entailed a changing crew of writers and directors, and was only released after Party intervention (10).

[9] Erich Fried, of Jewish descent, fled Austria in 1938 to escape the Nazis. He lived for most of the remainder of his life in England, where he died in 1988.

[10] Frances Goodrich's and Albert Hackett's stage version of the diary played successfully in East Germany between 1956–1961 with over 1,300 performances (Feinberg 125), though, as in the subsequent Hollywood film version, East German and American audiences received a somewhat de-Judaicized, universalistic version. The East German film announces at the outset that its purpose is to demonstrate those things that the play cannot. The film enjoyed considerable success in other European countries (East and West) and was at one point banned in West Germany (Heimann 84–86).

[11] The music serves as a leitmotif in the film, and occasions, for example, a flashback for Jakob's mother. Jakob believes the Nazis misuse this piece of the humanist heritage and that it can be reclaimed in postwar West Germany. The film argues, at least implicitly, that the humanist heritage can best be reclaimed in a socialist, neutral Germany.

[12] Ruth Bodenheim's father is a religious man and hence attached to "old legends" as his daughter notes. Nonetheless, he is able to anticipate the GDR, since he claims that "people are only strong when they come together to build a just, good world . . . . We [Jews] believe in such a world."

[13] She is freed by advancing Russian troops. In the least convincing scenes of the movie, she walks alone and unmolested, accompanied by triumphal

Russian music, through the Red Army. We learn that she is subsequently cared for in a Russian hospital.

[14] Diner 128. See also Thomas Heimann's discussion of East German films from the late 1950s and early 1960s (83–86). Heimann notes that in the GDR there were also important personages who had had close contact with Eichmann (84). On former Nazis in the GDR, see Herf, *Divided* 185–90. He writes: "There were many more former officials of the Nazi regime in West Germany than in the East. But the image of a pristine antifascist government cleansed of all ex-Nazis was more antifascist mythology than East German reality" (189).

[15] *Affaire Blum* is the first in a DEFA sub-genre dealing with miscarriages of justice (e.g., *Der Prozeß wird vertagt*, *Chronik eines Mordes*, *Der Mord, der nie verjährt*, *Mord am Montag*).

[16] O'Doherty, *Portrayal* 90. O'Doherty also notes that post-1953 East German discussions of the story do not mention the "Jewish" themes.

[17] Gertrud Koch notes that Holocaust films could be made but not shown in cinemas (64), but I have found no evidence of this.

[18] Here, as in *Professor Mamlock*, *Ehe im Schatten*, and *Affaire Blum*, the public encounters a "mixed" couple of Jew and non-Jew, most probably a device to render the Jew more acceptable.

[19] The novel was filmed by Frank Beyer in 1983.

[20] A traveling exhibition on the subject of *Wehrmacht* crimes has been the subject of much controversy in Germany. In 1997 and 1998 the exhibition occasioned massive protests and street fighting in western German Munich and eastern German Dresden.

[21] Translation of "Die Spur im Sand" from Scrase 21.

[22] Jan Koplowitz's novel *"Bohemia" — mein Schicksal* contains a similar narrative, with Peter Samuel leaving his family and the Jewish Community to join the Communists. Samuel survives the Holocaust, while his Jewish family does not.

[23] Wander's epigraph is of course itself problematic, suggesting as it does the Holocaust as a cleansing or purifying process.

[24] Becker once maintained that resistance is in fact the only theme of his novel, but not the kind that "has made an astonishing career" in literature about the Third Reich ("Resistance" 269–273).

[25] One also perceives elements of the standard East German Holocaust discourse in both book and film, for example in the (gentle) mocking of the prayers of an orthodox Jew. As we have noted, the book's narrator regrets the lack of Jewish resistance, and the film briefly includes some ominous Zionists.

[26] The title of Becker's novel can refer to either Mark or Arno, and one could in fact argue for Mark as the central figure.

[27] *Jewish* 344. Gilman however sees Mark as an East German positive hero, a reading with which I do not agree.

[28] See also Schultz 10–18, especially 14.

[29] J. Becker, *Bronstein's Children* 18. All subsequent citations are from the English translation and are in the text.

[30] See also Gilman's discussion in "Jüdische."

[31] See Eschwege, *Fremd* 180–83.

[32] Hans-Jörg Rother asserts that some of those scenes were censored ("Auftrag" 118).

[33] In the version I watched, distributed by Progress Film, the final voice-over is obviously interrupted, due either to censorship or, more likely, a technical problem. The film concludes with images of defaced Jewish gravestones and a voice (interrupted) that asserts that the past continues to return. It is not clear from the version I viewed whether the gravestones are in West Germany (which would be a standard East German conclusion) or in the East (which would have been quite sensational in 1966).

[34] For other references to the situation of Jews in Communism, see 368–69, 451–52, 507, 528–29, 678, 680.

[35] The actress's first lover is most probably a Communist who must flee the Nazis. As an act of defiance, the actress listens to American jazz music, denounced by the Nazis as "Jewish-Nigger music." During one scene when the actress is fleeing, she also encounters a group of black musicians.

[36] Seghers's father was a Jewish Elder in Mainz, and Seghers wrote her doctoral thesis on Jews in Rembrandt's painting. She did not publish it until 1981 in the GDR, after her 80th birthday. Biermann's father, a Jewish worker, died in Auschwitz. Except for a kind of identification with Heine, Biermann did not publicly concern himself with Judaism until the Gulf War. By then he had been living in the West for approximately 14 years.

[37] Numerous fairly traditional images of Jews continue to recirculate, for example the Jew as object of sexual desire or as tied to nature. Konrad Wolf brings many of these images together during a scene in *Sterne*, in which the face of the imprisoned Jewish woman (desired by the German soldier) is superimposed on the image of a stream while the soundtrack plays the cries of a newborn child.

[38] Provided, of course, that East German readers could gain access to his book, which was not printed in the GDR.

Epilogue: Stated Memory

*Some German intellectuals are call-
ing and searching for a new national
identity. But I'm afraid we cannot
look for any lost or new identity. We
have one and Auschwitz is part of it.*
                                    Peter Schneider

After the opening of the Wall in 1989, Jews in the GDR gained
freedom of expression and travel. Without reproach or censorship, they could establish international contacts, most importantly
with Israel. Nonetheless, for many East German Jews, German unification proved an occasion for uncertainty, even fear. Freedom of expression, for example, entails giving voice to right-wing diatribes
suppressed in the GDR. Eastern German Jews — and not they
alone — watched with apprehension as their fellow citizens (sometimes supported by West German right-wing groups) chanted nationalist slogans during burgeoning street demonstrations. They
witnessed an increase in raw violence, saw Africans and Vietnamese,
people of color brought to the GDR from "socialist brother countries," thrown from the S-Bahn trains in eastern Berlin or hunted
across East Berlin's Alexanderplatz like so many animals. They understood the message of firebomb attacks at the concentration camp
memorial sites in eastern Germany. On national television they
watched eastern Germans attack the quarters of asylum seekers in
Rostock and Hoyerswerda while police remained aloof. Such incidents did not occur in eastern Germany alone. In the West, in Solin-
gen and Mölln, Turkish homes were set ablaze and the inhabitants
perished. Germany is the only civilized country in the world, wrote
Henryk Broder in 1993, where pogroms are taking place every week
(11–12).
    In an essay written after 1989 and remarkably free of nostalgia,
Peter Kirchner enumerated some reasons why many East German
Jews, or people of Jewish descent, had supported the GDR. Having
been persecuted by the Nazis, they wanted to identify with a state
led by those who had fought their persecutors. They applauded the
eradication of the ostensible political and economic bases for fascism,

the purging of the judiciary and the educational system of Nazi elements, the rigorous suppression of right wing activity and discourse. Frank Stern writes: "In the end, in a strange historical twist, it was very often the East Germans of Jewish origin who still adhered to the antifascist notion, while its contents and meaning had long eroded" (61). Kirchner admits that many of the revelations since 1989 have seriously weakened previous arguments in favor of the GDR, and he concedes that even before 1989 there were aspects of the system Jews chose to overlook (33; 29).

In this study I have attempted to demonstrate that regardless of the degree of sincerity of the people involved, the East German state-organized discourse in general constructed a Holocaust memory that served political ends, specifically the legitimation of the GDR. East German historiography organized itself around a master teleological narrative designed to celebrate the Soviet Union and its German Communist allies in their struggle against German fascism. As Eve Rosenhaft notes, this celebration disguised "a process by which some aspects of the resistance [were] selected and instrumentalized at the expense of others" (371). Furthermore, a *grand récit* driven by economic determinism cannot explain racially-motivated genocide, and the Jewish catastrophe long lingered on the margins of most aspects of East German life.

The Holocaust could not be airbrushed from history, but it could be interpreted according to state interest. By explaining the Holocaust as the work of certain historically declining classes, by perceiving the Second World War as the triumph of the historically more advanced Soviet Union over fascist Germany, the East Germans could contain and "state" the Jewish catastrophe within a comfortingly progress-oriented teleology. Visiting Auschwitz soon after the Second World War, Stephan Hermlin wrote:

> Auschwitz is the monument around which a people gathers in order to commemorate its suffering and with tenfold, no hundredfold strength to fight for earthly happiness. Auschwitz, that inextinguishable stain on a group of people that sank into bestiality, on a system that in all its forms must unhesitatingly give way to socialist humanism, has become the honor of the Polish nation. The furious reconstruction of Warsaw and the ruins of the crematorium belong together. How safely the dead rest in this land that continually commemorates the victims, in order to fight more resolutely for life, in order to measure the distance that divides

yesterday from today, and which will divide today from tomorrow. ("Auschwitz" 89)

Hermlin's images of the dead lying peacefully under the rubble recurs in his writing from that time, for example in "Die Zeit der Gemeinsamkeit," where Jonathan Ross terms the description "grotesque" (224). And Hermlin's determinedly optimistic millenarianism ignores, for example, postwar Polish pogroms. But his figurative language structures and "explains" the genocide. The antifascist explanation served as a state supported, and supporting, foundation myth, but one can imagine that for individuals such as Hermlin, who had been persecuted during the war, it was psychologically enabling. Perhaps for that reason he actively supported that foundation myth, both in his writing and in the at times overtly fictional construction of his own autobiography. In this way, as Dan Diner writes in a similar context, the horror could be brought under control (131).

Refusing to recognize itself in any way as a successor state to the Nazis, the GDR sought to free itself of the historical baggage that so noticeably weighed on the Federal Republic. The issue of restitution payments made by the Federal Republic to Israel — and from which West Germany benefited by a growth in international stature — was instrumentalized in various phases by the GDR from the 1950s to the 1990s: to silence inner opposition; to attain standing with Arab states; to variously attack or curry favor with the United States; and, after years of hostility, to attempt to establish ties with Israel. Equating Zionism with fascism, the GDR supplied Arab states and the PLO with weapons and military training, so that once again German know-how helped kill Jews. In a curious but ultimately logical displacement, self-styled German "antifascists" supported the struggle against Jewish "fascists." The former group included anti-Zionist antifascists of Jewish descent. Wolf Biermann for example asserts: "Markus Wolf [brother of the filmmaker Konrad], one-time general in the dreaded Ministry for State Security and head of East German foreign intelligence, is also a Jew. His GDR systematically supported Israel's mortal enemies by training Iraqi officers in chemical warfare and serving as a base of operations for Arab terrorists" (105).

In its productions of *Nathan der Weise*, as in every other aspect of its Jewish-related discourse, the GDR construed the Holocaust as a misstep in the inexorable march toward Enlightenment and Communism. Whereas Lyotard compares the Holocaust to an earthquake so powerful that it destroyed all instruments of measure, the GDR proceeded as though the instruments were still intact. East Germany in effect conducted an elaborate charade according to which the German-Jewish symbiosis, and the accompanying project of assimilation, continued as if there had been no earthquake. Small wonder that the dialectic of Enlightenment made itself felt with a vengeance: when useful to the state, a "Jew" — religious or assimilated — remained a "Jew." (I am using "Jew" here in Lyotard's sense, as a social construct). Anti-Semitism did not disappear in the classless society either, as even some old comrades, those who most insistently invoked a "time together," admitted after 1989. In 1992 Stephan Hermlin noted in an interview:

> In the Party I made some very close friends, but I met yet more people that I count among my worst enemies. These comrades confronted me from the very beginning with a senseless, irrational enmity. I often asked myself: What is it about me? What has such an unpleasant effect on these people? *What could that have been?* I have a suspicion — to be sure, a somewhat unsettling one . . . . *Anti-Semitism?* Yes. *Why?* Those are things that for a long, long time one does not want to admit. One prettifies reality in order to suit oneself. Many people with a similar background to mine had similar experiences. Anna Seghers for example . . . .
>
> (Cited in Groehler, "Juden" 54)

Jeffrey Herf points out that East Germany was not an anti-Semitic state in the sense that Nazi Germany had been; hatred of Jews was not a guiding principle. But it was willing to adopt the language of traditional European anti-Semitism (*Divided* 384). And its refusal to acknowledge the magnitude of the Jewish catastrophe, its failure to pay restitution, its persecution of citizens of Jewish descent in the 1950s, its pressure on remaining East German Jewish leaders, its support of Israel's enemies, or its instrumentalization of Holocaust memory were not actions friendly to Jews.

As readers of Foucault, however, we should remember that power is not monolithic and always negative. If East German antifascist discourse was in many ways a legitimizing myth that too often impeded a painful confrontation with the past, it was also, for many East Germans, an "ethical category" (Diner 125), a "basic content in [their] lives, aspirations, and activities" (Stern 64). Günter Kunert declared: "This prescribed antifascism: Yes, well I lived through all that and for me it wasn't at all prescribed. I believe that this is a very vital point that is too often misunderstood" (Cited in Bathrick 12). Many East Germans who participated in commemoration activities and other acts of memory did so out of genuine conviction, even if that activity ultimately served less than noble state purposes. As Olaf Groehler admonishes, the magnitude and fervor of, say, the 1988 East German commemorations of the so-called *Kristallnacht* cannot be attributed solely to the East German desire to gain Most Favored Nation trade status with the United States ("Holocaust" 62). Schoolchildren who visited concentration camp memorials, or who were visited by concentration camp survivors, were less likely to deny the Holocaust, regardless of the stories told by the memorials or the survivors. East German leaders were Stalinists, but some, like Erich Honecker, were also bona fide antifascist heroes. The state celebrated such antifascists as Walter Bartel, or Stephan Hermlin, or Erich Honecker as role models. Such things mattered. But it also mattered that Bartel and Hermlin could not tell their whole story, and embellished the stories they did tell.

Many cultural practitioners participated in the construction and maintenance of the state-supporting antifascist narrative, as such examples as Bruno Apitz's *Nackt unter Wölfen* or Frank Beyer's film of that novel demonstrate. East German emplotments of, for example, the Warsaw ghetto revolt, that quintessential act of Jewish resistance, project into the uprising a moment of socialist resistance and teleology (for example, Stephan Hermlin's "Die Zeit der Gemeinsamkeit," Rolf Schneider's *Geschichte von Moischele*, Rainer Kerndl's *Die seltsame Reise des Alois Fingerlein*, Stefan Heym's *Ahasver*).[1] The most egregious excesses of such a rhetoric, for example in Konrad Wolf's film *Professor Mamlock*, entails blaming those Jews who did not resist with the Communists for their own death.

Yet from within the master narrative maintained by the East German state, such writers as Heinz Knobloch, in his *Herr Moses in Berlin*, interrogated the Marxist theory of anti-Semitism. Kurt Maetzig, Johannes Bobrowski, and Günter Kunert, among many others, worked to create a discourse of mourning in literature and film. Jurek Becker's *Jakob der Lügner*, and Frank Beyer's film, also participate in mourning without the requisite teleological triumph, and they subversively reorder the meaning of resistance. Konrad Wolf's film *Sterne* presents the confrontation of an ordinary German soldier with the Holocaust. Jurek Becker's *Der Boxer* and *Bronsteins Kinder* probe the question of what it means to be "Jewish" in (East) Germany. These works were generated by and through the East German discourses of antifascism and the Holocaust, which means to be sure that within the East German context, the regime could, and did, employ them as a legitimating gesture. But as works of art they cannot be contained within that paradigm alone, and they present some of the more important postwar German cultural confrontations with the Holocaust. These works of the imagination will continue to figure in any attempt to reconfigure, or reimagine, the constellation of German identity.

Notes

[1] Jonathan Ross's statement that "'Die Zeit der Gemeinsamkeit' is, as far as I can ascertain, the only work of German fiction to focus on the events of the Warsaw Ghetto Uprising" (256) needs some modification. The works I mention do not focus entirely on the uprising, but the revolt does play an important role in each.

Works Cited

Adling, Wilfried. "Nachwort." Friedrich Wolf. *Professor Mamlock*. Leipzig: Reclam, 1980. 77–84.

Ammer, Thomas. "DDR und Judentum. 50 Jahre nach den November-pogromen." *Deutschland Archiv* 22.1 (1989): 17–23.

Anderson, Benedict. *Imagined Communities. Reflections on the Origin and Spread of Nationalism*. London: Verso, 1983.

Angress, Ruth. "A 'Jewish Problem' in German Postwar Fiction." *Modern Judaism* 5 (1988): 215–133.

Apitz, Bruno. *Nackt unter Wölfen*. Halle: Mitteldeutscher Verlag, 1958.

Arndt, Theodor et al., eds. *Juden in der DDR*. Duisburg: E.J. Brill, 1988.

Bartel, Walter. *Deutschland in der Zeit der faschistischen Diktatur 1933–1945*. Berlin: Volk und Wissen, 1956.

——. *Fernstudium der Lehrer. Geschichte. 20. Lehrbrief. Deutschland in der Zeit der faschistischen Diktatur (1933 bis 1945)*. Berlin: Volk und Wissen, 1955.

Bathrick, David. *The Powers of Speech. The Politics of Culture in the GDR*. Lincoln: U of Nebraska P, 1995.

Becher, Johannes R. *Der Weg nach Füssen. Schauspiel in fünf Akten*. J. R. Becher. *Gesammelte Werke*. Vol. VIII. Berlin: Aufbau, 1970. 705–804.

Becker, Jurek. *Der Boxer*. Frankfurt: Suhrkamp, 1979.

——. *Bronstein's Children*. Trans. Leila Vennewitz. NY: Harcourt Brace Jovanovich, 1988.

——. *Bronsteins Kinder*. Frankfurt: Suhrkamp, 1986.

——. *Jakob der Lügner*. Frankfurt: Suhrkamp, 1982.

——. *Jakob the Liar*. Trans. Leila Vennewitz. NY: Schocken, 1990.

——. "Resistance in *Jakob der Lügner*." *Seminar* 14.4 (1983): 269–273.

Becker, Stefan. "Zur künstlerischen Gestaltung der Gedenkstätte Sachsenhausen." *Von der Erinnerung zum Monument. Die Entstehungsgeschichte der Nationalen Mahn- und Gedenkstätte Sachsenhausen*. Ed. Günter Morsch. Berlin: Hentrich, 1996. 284–288.

Benz, Wolfgang. "Antisemitismus in Deutschland. Tradition und Trends seit der Vereinigung." *Antisemitismus in Osteuropa. Aspekte einer historischen Kontinuität.* Ed. Peter Bettelheim et al. Vienna: Picus, 1992. 25–39.

——, ed. *Jahrbuch für Antisemitismusforschung 2.* Frankfurt: Campus, 1993.

——, ed. *Zwischen Antisemitismus und Philosemitismus. Juden in der Bundesrepublik.* Berlin: Metropol, 1991.

Bhabha, Homi K., ed. *Nation and Narration.* NY: Routledge, 1990.

Bier, Jean-Paul. *Auschwitz et les nouvelles littératures allemandes.* Brussels: Ed. de l'Université, 1979.

Biermann, Wolf. "Jewish Identity— An East German Dimension." *Speaking Out. Jewish Voices from United Germany.* Ed. Susan Stern. Chicago: edition q, 1995. 102–15.

Bobrowski, Johannes. "An den Chassid Barkan." *Werke I* 95.

——. "An Nelly Sachs." *Werke I* 119.

——. "Auf den jüdischen Händler A.S." *Werke I* 15.

——. "Else Lasker-Schüler." *Werke I* 117.

——. "Die ersten zwei Sätze für ein Deutschlandbuch." *Werke IV* 89–90.

——. "Gertrud Kolmar." *Werke I* 116.

——. "Die Heimat des Malers Chagall." *Werke I* 56.

——. "Holunderblüte." *Werke I* 94.

——. *Levin's Mill.* Trans. Janet Cropper. London: Calder and Boyars, 1970.

——. *Levins Mühle. Werke III* 7–223.

——. "Mäusefest." *Werke IV* 47–49.

——. "Der Tänzer Malige." *Werke IV* 164–169.

——. *Werke,* vol. I-IV. Ed. Eberhard Haufe. Berlin: Union, 1987.

Bock, Wolfgang. "DDR-Justiz und Strafverfahren wegen nationalsozialistischer Gewaltverbrechen. Eine Erläuterung der Rahmenbedingungen." *Erinnerung. Zur Gegenwart des Holocaust in Deutschland-West und Deutschland-Ost.* Ed. Bernhard Moltmann et al. Frankfurt: Haag + Herchen, 1993. 119–127.

Borneman, John and Jeffrey M. Peck. *Sojourners. The Return of German Jews and the Question of Identity.* Lincoln: U of Nebraska P, 1995.

Böttcher, Kurt et al. *Romanführer A-Z.* Vol. II, no. 1. Berlin: Volk und Wissen, 1974.

Broder, Henryk. *Erbarmen mit den Deutschen.* Hamburg: Hoffmann und Campe, 1993.

Brecht, Bertolt. *Furcht und Elend des Dritten Reiches.* B. Brecht. *Gesammelte Werke in 20 Bänden.* Vol. III. Frankfurt: Suhrkamp, 1976. 1073–1193.

Bredel, Willi. "Das schweigende Dorf." W. Bredel. *Gesammelte Werke in Einzelausgaben.* Vol. XI. 2nd ed. Berlin: Aufbau, 1981. 217–265.

Burgauer, Erica. *Zwischen Erinnerung und Verdrängung. Juden in Deutschland nach 1945.* Reinbeck: Rowohlt, 1993.

Buruma, Ian. *The Wages of Guilt.* London: Jonathan Cape, 1994.

Childs, David. *The GDR: Moscow's German Ally.* London: George Allen and Unwin, 1983.

Cohn, Michael. *The Jews in Germany, 1945–1993. The Building of a Minority.* Westport: Praeger, 1994.

Combe, Sonja. "DDR: Die letzten Tage der deutsch-jüdischen Symbiose." *Erinnerung. Zur Gegenwart des Holocaust in Deutschland-West und Deutschland-Ost.* Ed. Bernhard Moltmann et al. Frankfurt: Haag + Herchen, 1993. 137–148.

Corino, Carl. *Außen Marmor, innen Gips: Die Legenden des Stephan Hermlin.* Düsseldorf: ECON, 1996.

Danzinger, Carl Jakob. *Die Partei hat immer recht. Autobiographischer Roman.* Stuttgart: Werner Gebühr, 1976.

Davis, Geoffrey V. *Arnold Zweig in der DDR. Entstehung und Bearbeitung der Romane* Die Feuerpause, Das Eis bricht, *und* Traum ist teuer. Bonn: Bouvier, 1977.

Demetz, Peter. *After the Fires. Recent Writing in the Germanies, Austria, and Switzerland.* New York: Harcourt Brace Jovanovich, 1986.

Deutschkron, Inge. *Israel und die Deutschen. Das schwierige Verhältnis.* Cologne: Verlag Wissenschaft und Politik, 1991.

Dietzel, Ulrich, ed. *Stephan Hermlin. Äußerungen 1944–1982.* Berlin: Aufbau, 1983.

Diner, Dan. "On the Ideology of Antifascism." *New German Critique* 67 (1996): 123–132.

Dittmar, Peter. "DDR und Israel (I). Ambivalenz einer Nicht-Beziehung." *Deutschland Archiv* 10.7 (1977): 736–754.

——. "DDR und Israel (II). Ambivalenz einer Nicht-Beziehung." *Deutschland Archiv* 10.8 (1977): 848–861.

Drobisch, Klaus et al. *Juden unterm Hakenkreuz. Verfolgung und Ausrottung der deutschen Juden. 1933–1945.* Berlin: Verlag der Wissenschaften, 1973.

Eckert, Rainer. "Ende eines Mythos oder Mitbringsel in das vereinigte Deutschland? Der DDR-Antifaschismus nach der Herbstrevolution von 1989." *Brandenburgische Gedenkstätten für die Verfolgten des NS-Regimes. Perspektiven, Kontroversen und internationale Vergleiche.* Ed. Ministerium für Wissenschaft, Forschung und Kultur des Landes Brandenburg. Berlin: Edition Hentrich, 1992. 86–94.

Edel, Peter. *Die Bilder des Zeugen Schattmann. Ein Roman über deutsche Vergangenheit und Gegenwart.* 2d ed. Berlin: Verlag der Nation, 1969.

Elsässer, Jürgen. *Antisemitismus — das alte Gesicht des neuen Deutschland.* Berlin: Dietz, 1992.

Endlich, Stephanie. "Geschichte und Zukunft der NS-Gedenkstätten in der vormaligen DDR." *Aufbau nach dem Untergang. Deutsch-Jüdische Geschichte nach 1945. In memoriam Heinz Galinskis.* Ed. Andreas Nachama und Julius H. Schoeps. Berlin: Argon, 1992. 107–120.

Eschwege, Helmut. *Fremd unter meinesgleichen. Erinnerungen eines Dresdner Juden.* Berlin: Links, 1991.

——. "Die jüdische Bevölkerung der Jahre nach der Kapitulation Hitlerdeutschlands auf dem Gebiet der DDR bis zum Jahre 1953." *Juden in der DDR.* Ed. Theodor Arndt et al. Duisburg: E.J. Brill, 1988. 63–100.

——, ed. *Kennzeichen J. Bilder, Dokumente, Berichte zur Geschichte der Verbrechen des Hitlerfaschismus an den deutschen Juden 1933–1945.* Berlin: Deutscher Verlag der Wissenschaften, 1966.

Feinberg, Anat. *Wiedergutmachung im Programm. Jüdisches Schicksal im deutschen Nachkriegsdrama.* Cologne: Prometh, 1988.

Fischer, Barbara. "Residues of Otherness. On Jewish Emancipation during the Age of German Enlightenment." *Insiders and Outsiders. Jewish and Gentile Culture in Germany and Austria.* Ed. Dagmar Lorenz and Gabriele Weinberger. Detroit: Wayne State UP, 1994. 30–38.

Fischer, Peter. "Ich wollte ja nie Funktionär werden." *Zwischen Thora und Trabant. Juden in der DDR.* Ed. Vincent von Wroblewsky. Berlin: Aufbau, 1993. 63–81.

Friedländer, Saul. *Memory, History, and the Extermination of the Jews of Europe.* Bloomington: Indiana UP, 1993.

Frisch, Max. *Andorra. Stück in zwölf Bildern.* Frankfurt: Suhrkamp, 1961.

Füllberg-Stolberg, Claus and Martina Jung, Renate Riebe, Martina Scheitenberger, eds. *Frauen in Konzentrationslagern. Bergen-Belsen. Ravensbrück.* Bremen: Editions Temmen, 1994.

Genin, Salomea. "Rückkehr? Wie ich in der DDR aus einer Kommunistin zu einer Jüdin wurde." *Das Exil der kleinen Leute. Alltagserfahrungen deutscher Juden in der Emigration.* Ed. Wolfgang Benz. Munich: C.H. Beck, 1991. 309–326.

Geschichte. Lehrbuch für Klasse 9. 7th ed. Berlin: Volk und Wissen, 1976.

Geschichte. Lehrbuch für Klasse 9. 4th ed. Berlin: Volk und Wissen, 1987 [1984 edition].

Gilman, Sander. *Jewish Self-Hatred. Anti-Semitism and the Hidden Language of the Jews.* Baltimore: Johns Hopkins UP, 1986.

——. "Jüdische Literaten und deutsche Literatur." *Zeitschrift für deutsche Philologie* 107.2 (1988): 270–294.

Giordano, Ralph. *Die zweite Schuld oder Von der Last, Deutscher zu sein.* Hamburg: Rasch und Röhring, 1987.

Goldhagen, Daniel Jonah. *Hitler's Willing Executioners. Ordinary Germans and the Holocaust.* New York: Alfred A. Knopf, 1996.

Goschler, Constantin. "Paternalismus und Verweigerung — Die DDR und die Wiedergutmachung für Verfolgte des Nationalsozialismus." *Jahrbuch für Antisemitismusforschung 2.* Ed. Wolfgang Benz. Frankfurt: Campus, 1993. 93–117.

Gossweiler, Kurt. "Aus dem Arsenal des Kalten Krieges." *Konkret* 8 (1992): 46–50.

Grabitz, Helge. "Die Verfolgung von NS-Verbrechen in der Bundesrepublik Deutschland, der Deutschen Demokratischen Republik und Österreich." *Der Umgang mit dem Holocaust. Europa — USA — Israel.* Ed. Rolf Steininger. Vienna: Böhlau, 1994. 198–220.

Gregor-Dellin, Martin. *Jakob Haferglanz.* Munich: Piper, 1986.

Groehler, Olaf. "Der Holocaust in der Geschichtsschreibung der DDR." *Zweierlei Bewältigung. Vier Beiträge über den Umgang mit der NS-Vergangenheit in den beiden deutschen Staaten.* Ed. Ulrich Herbert and Olaf Groehler. Hamburg: Ergebnisse, 1992. 41–66.

——. "Juden erkennen wir nicht an." *Konkret* 3 (1993): 50–54.

——. "Der Umgang mit dem Holocaust in der DDR." *Der Umgang mit dem Holocaust. Europa — USA — Israel.* Ed. Rolf Steininger. Vienna: Böhlau, 1994. 233–245.

——. "Der Umgang mit dem Holocaust in der Sowjetischen Besatzungszone und in der Deutschen Demokratischen Republik." Paper delivered
at the German Studies Association (GSA) conference, Washington,
D.C., November 1993.

Grunenberg, Antonia. *Antifaschismus. Ein deutscher Mythos*. Reinbeck:
Rowohlt, 1993.

Hage, Volker, "Hinter dem Rücken des Vaters." *Deutsche Literatur 1986*.
Ed. Volker Hage. Stuttgart: Reclam, 1987. 331–42.

Heimann, Thomas. "Von Stahl und Menschen. 1953 bis 1960." *Schwarzweiß und Farbe. DEFA-Dokumentarfilme 1946–92*. Ed. Günter Jordan
and Ralf Schenk. Potsdam: Jovis, 1996. 48–91.

Hein, Christoph. *Passage*. In *Theater der Zeit* 5 (1987): 54–64.

Herbert, Ulrich. *Fremdarbeiter. Politik und Praxis des "Ausländer-Ein-
satzes" in der Kriegswirtschaft des Dritten Reiches*. Bonn: J.H.W. Dietz,
1985.

Herbert, Ulrich and Olaf Groehler. *Zweierlei Bewältigung. Vier Beiträge
über den Umgang mit der NS-Vergangenheit in den beiden deutschen
Staaten*. Hamburg: Ergebnisse, 1992.

——. "Zweierlei Bewältigung." Herbert and Groehler, 7–27.

Herf, Jeffrey. *Divided Memory. The Nazi Past in the Two Germanys*. Cambridge: Harvard UP, 1997.

——. "East German Communists and the Jewish Question. The Case of
Paul Merker." Washington: German Historical Institute, 1994.

——. "German Communism, the Discourse of 'Antifascist Resistance,'
and the Jewish Catastrophe." *Resistance against the Third Reich 1933–
1990*. Ed. Michael Geyer. Chicago: U of Chicago P, 1994. 257–294.

Hermlin, Stephan. *Abendlicht*. Berlin: Klaus Wagenbach, 1979.

——. "Die Asche von Birkenau." S. Hermlin. *Gedichte und Nachdichtun-
gen*. Berlin: Aufbau, 1990. 124–26.

——. "Auschwitz ist unvergessen." *Stephan Hermlin. Äußerungen 1944–
1982*. Ed. Ulrich Dietzel. Berlin: Aufbau, 1983. 85–89.

——. *Die erst Reihe*. Berlin: Neues Leben, 1985. Fifth printing.

——. *Evening Light*. Trans. Paul F. Dvorak. San Francisco: Fjord Press,
1983.

——. "Hier liegen die Gesetzgeber." *Stephan Hermlin. Äußerungen
1944–1982*. Ed. Ulrich Dietzel. Berlin: Aufbau, 1983. 99–104.

——. "Wo sind wir zu Hause? Gespräch mit Klaus Wagenbach." *Stephan Hermlin. Äußerungen 1944–1982*. Ed. Ulrich Dietzel. Berlin: Aufbau, 1983. 396–408.

——. "Die Zeit der Gemeinsamkeit." Berlin: Volk und Welt, 1949.

Herzberg, Wolfgang. *Überleben heißt Erinnern. Lebensgeschichten deutscher Juden*. Berlin: Aufbau, 1990.

Heukenkamp, Ursula. "Jüdische Figuren in der Nachkriegsliteratur der SBZ und DDR." *Erinnerung. Zur Gegenwart des Holocaust in Deutschland-West und Deutschland-Ost*. Ed. Bernhard Moltmann et al. Frankfurt: Haag + Herchen, 1993. 189–203.

Heym, Stefan. *Ahasver*. Munich: Bertelsmann, 1981.

——. *Collin*. Munich: Bertelsmann, 1979.

——. *Lassalle*. Munich: Bechtle, 1969.

——. *Nachruf*. Munich: Bertelsmann, 1988.

——. *Die Papiere des Andreas Lenz*. Leipzig: List, 1963.

——. *Radek*. Munich: Bertelsmann, 1995.

——. "Schreiben nach Auschwitz." S. Heym. *Stalin verläßt den Raum. Politische Publizistik*. Leipzig: Reclam, 1990. 227–235.

——. *Schwarzenberg*. Munich: Bertelsmann, 1988.

——. *The Wandering Jew*. New York: Holt, Rinehart, and Winston, 1984.

Heymann, Stefan. *Marxismus und Rassenfrage*. Berlin: Dietz, 1948.

Hirsch, Rudolf. *Patria Israel*. Rudolstadt: Greifenverlag, 1983.

——, and Rosmarie Schuder. *Der gelbe Fleck. Wurzeln und Wirkungen des Judenhasses in der deutschen Geschichte*. Berlin: Rütten und Loening, 1989.

Hochhuth, Rolf. *Der Stellvertreter*. Reinbek: Rowohlt, 1963.

Hoffman, Charles. *Grey Dawn*. New York: Harper Collins, 1992.

Honigmann, Barbara. "Marina Roza." B. Honigmann. *Roman von einem Kinde*. Darmstadt: Luchterhand, 1986. 99–108.

Honigmann, Peter. "Über den Umgang mit Juden und jüdischer Geschichte in der DDR." *Juden in der DDR*. Ed. Theodor Arndt et al. Duisburg: E.J. Brill, 1988. 101–124.

Huyssen, Andreas. "Monument and Memory in a Postmodern Age." *The Art of Memory. Holocaust Memorials in History*. Ed. James Young. New York: Prestel, 1993. 9–17.

Horkheimer, Max and Theodor Adorno. *Dialektik der Aufklärung.* Frankfurt: Suhrkamp, 1981.

Interview of author with Silvia Nickel, Sachsenhausen Memorial Site, June 1993.

Interview of author with Harry Stein, Buchenwald Memorial Site, June 1993.

Jacobeit, Sigrid and Lieselotte Thomo-Heinrich, eds. *Kreuzweg Ravensbrück. Lebensbilder antifaschistischer Wiederstandskämpferinnen.* Leipzig: Verlag für die Frau, 1987.

Jarausch, Konrad H. "The Failure of East German Antifascism: Some Ironies of History as Politics." *German Studies Review* 14.1 (1991): 85–102.

Jarmartz, Klaus, ed. *Ravensbrücker Ballade oder Faschismusbewältigung in der DDR.* Berlin: Aufbau, 1992.

Jay, Martin. "The Jews and the Frankfurt School. Critical Theory's Analysis of Anti-Semitism." *Germans and Jews since the Holocaust.* Ed. Anton Rabinbach and Jack Zipes. New York: Holmes and Meier, 1986. 287–301.

Johnson, Uwe. *Mutmaßungen über Jakob.* Frankfurt: Suhrkamp, 1959.

Joos, Rudolf and Isolde I. Mozer, eds. *Deutsche Geschichte bis 1945. Ereignisse und Entwicklungen. Filmanalytische Materialien.* Frankfurt: Gemeinschaftswerk der Evangelischen Publizistik, 1988.

Jordan, Günter and Ralf Schenk, eds. *Schwarzweiß und Farbe. DEFA-Dokumentarfilme 1946–92.* Potsdam: Jovis, 1996.

Jüdische Gemeinden der DDR, eds. *Gedenke! Vergiß nie! 40. Jahrestag des faschistischen "Kristallnacht"-Pogroms.* Berlin: Union, 1979.

Jüdisches Historisches Institut Warschau, ed. *Faschismus-Getto-Massenmord.* 2nd ed. Berlin: Rütten und Loening, 1961.

Jung, Thomas. "Yellow Star and Empty Space — Perception/Reception of the Holocaust in the GDR." Unpublished paper delivered at the DEFA Film Conference, University of Massachusetts, October 1997.

Kahane, Anetta. "Ich durfte, die anderen mußten." *Zwischen Thora und Trabant. Juden in der DDR.* Ed. Vincent von Wroblewsky. Berlin: Aufbau, 1993. 124–145.

Kahn, Siegbert. *Antisemitismus und Rassenhetze. Eine Übersicht über ihre Entwicklung in Deutschland.* Berlin: Dietz, 1948.

——. "Dokumente des Kampfes der revolutionären deutschen Arbeiterbewegung gegen Antisemitismus und Judenverfolgung." *Beiträge zur Geschichte der deutschen Arbeiterbewegung* 2.3 (1960): 552–64.

Kant, Hermann. *Der Aufenthalt.* Berlin: Rütten und Loening, 1977.

Kaplan, Marion. "What is 'Religion' among Jews in Contemporary Germany?" *Reemerging Jewish Culture in Germany. Life and Literature since 1989.* Ed. Sander Gilman and Karen Remmler. New York: New York UP, 1994. 77–112.

Kaufmann, Walter. *Drei Reisen ins Gelobte Land.* Leipzig: F.A. Brockhaus, 1980.

Kaul, Friedrich. *Der Fall Eichmann.* Berlin: Das neue Berlin, 1963.

Keller, Herbert. *Begegnung 57. Ein Spiel über ein Stück deutsche Wirklichkeit.* Leipzig: Friedrich Hofmeister, 1960.

Kerndl, Rainer. *Die seltsame Reise des Alois Fingerlein.* R. Kerndl. *Stücke.* Berlin: Henschelverlag, 1972. 173–248.

Kessler, Mario. "Zwischen Repression und Toleranz. Die SED-Politik und die Juden (1949–1967)." *Historische DDR-Forschung. Aufsätze und Studien.* Ed. Jürgen Kocka. Berlin: Akademie, 1993. 149–167.

Kipphardt, Heinar. *Bruder Eichmann.* Reinbeck: Rowohlt, 1983.

Kirchner, Peter. "Die jüdische Minorität in der ehemaligen DDR." *Zwischen Antisemitismus und Philosemitismus. Juden in der Bundesrepublik.* Ed. Wolfgang Benz. Berlin: Metropol, 1991. 29–38.

Knigge, Volkhard. "Antifaschistischer Widerstand und Holocaust. Zur Geschichte der KZ-Gedenkstätten in der DDR." *Erinnerung. Zur Gegenwart des Holocaust in Deutschland-West und Deutschland-Ost.* Ed. Bernhard Moltmann et al. Frankfurt: Haag + Herchen, 1993. 67–77.

Knobloch, Heinz. *Herr Moses in Berlin. Auf den Spuren eines Menschenfreundes.* Berlin: Der Morgen, 1979.

Kogon, Eugen. *Der SS-Staat. Das System der deutschen Konzentrationslager.* Munich: Kindler, 1974.

Koch, Gertrud. "On the Disappearance of the Dead Among the Living — The Holocaust and the Confusion of Identities in the Films of Konrad Wolf." *New German Critique* 60 (1993): 57–75.

Komitee der Antifaschistischen Widerstandskämpfer in der DDR, ed. *Damals in Sachsenhausen. Solidarität und Widerstand im Konzentrationslager Sachsenhausen.* 2nd. ed. Berlin: Deutscher Verlag der Wissenschaften 1967, 1970.

——, ed. *Sachsenhausen. Dokumente, Aussagen, Forschungsergebnisse und Erlebnisberichte über das ehemalige Konzentrationslager Sachsenhausen.* Berlin: Deutscher Verlag der Wissenschaften, 1974, 1977, 1982.

Koonz, Claudia. "Between Memory and Oblivion: Concentration Camps in German Memory." *Commemorations. The Politics of National Identity.* Ed. John R. Gillis. Princeton: Princeton UP, 1994. 258–280.

——. "Germany's Buchenwald. Whose Shrine? Whose Memory?" *The Art of Memory. Holocaust Memorials in History.* Ed. James Young. New York: Prestel, 1993. 111–119.

Koplowitz, Jan. *"Bohemia." Mein Schicksal. Eine Familiengeschichte.* 2nd ed. Halle: Mitteldeutscher Verlag, 1979.

——. *Karfunkel und der Taschendieb.* J. Koplowitz. *Drei Geschichten.* Halle: Mitteldeutscher Verlag, 1988.

Korey, William. *The Soviet Cage. Anti-Semitism in Russia.* New York: Viking, 1973.

Kuczynski, Jürgen. *Dialog mit meinem Urenkel. Neunzehn Briefe und ein Tagebuch.* Berlin: Aufbau, 1983.

——. "Wo wäre das anders gewesen?" *Konkret* 8 (1992): 44–46.

Kuhn, Fritz. *Kredit bei Nibelungen. Eine tragische Komödie in acht Bildern.* Berlin: Henschelverlag, 1961.

Kühnrich, Heinz. *Judenmörder Eichmann. Kein Fall der Vergangenheit.* Berlin: Dietz, 1961.

——. *Der KZ-Staat.* Berlin: Dietz, 1960.

Kunert, Günter. "Oranienburger Strasse 28." G. Kunert. *Ziellose Umtriebe.* Berlin: Aufbau, 1979. 206–212.

——. "Rohstoff, unsichtbar." *Aufbau nach dem Untergang. Deutsch-Jüdische Geschichte nach 1945. In memoriam Heinz Galinski.* Ed. Andreas Nachama and Julius H. Schoeps. Berlin: Argon, 1992. 248–251.

Kwiet, Konrad. "Historians of the German Democratic Republic on Antisemitism and Persecution." *Leo Baeck Institute Yearbook* 21 (1976): 173–198.

——, and Konrad Eschwege. *Selbstbehauptung und Widerstand. Deutsche Juden im Kampf um Existenz und Menschenwürde. 1933–1945.* Hamburg: Christians, 1984.

Lagergemeinschaft Buchenwald-Dora der Bundesrepublik Deutschland, ed. *Buchenwald. Ein Konzentrationslager.* Frankfurt: Röderberg, 1986.

Lauckner, Nancy. "The Treatment of Holocaust Themes in GDR Fiction from the Late 1960s to the Mid-1970s: A Survey." *Studies in GDR Culture and Society.* Ed. Margy Gerber et al. Washington: UP of America, 1981. 141–154.

Lederer, Gerda et al. "Autoritarismus unter Jugendlichen der ehemaligen DDR." *Deutschland Archiv* 24.6 (1991): 587–596.

Lehrbuch für den Geschichtsunterricht. 8. Schuljahr. Berlin: Volk und Wissen, 1951.

Lehrbuch für den Geschichtsunterricht. 8. Schuljahr. Berlin: Volk und Wissen, 1954.

Lehrbuch für Geschichte der 10. Klasse der Oberschule und der erweiterten Oberschule. Berlin: Volk und Wissen, 1961.

Lehrbuch für Geschichte der 9. Klasse der Oberschule. Berlin: Volk und Wissen, 1963.

Lehrbuch für Geschichte. 10. Klasse, Teil I. Oberschule und erweiterte Oberschule. Berlin: Volk und Wissen, 1965.

Lehrbuch für Geschichte. 9. Klasse. Berlin: Volk und Wissen, 1969.

"Lehren aus dem Prozess gegen das Verschwörerzentrum Slánský." *Dokumente der Sozialistischen Einheitspartei Deutschlands.* Vol. IV. Berlin: Dietz, 1954. 199–219.

Lessing, Gotthold Ephraim. *Nathan der Weise.* Stuttgart: Reclam, 1995.

Lorenz, Heinz. "Edel, Peter." *Romanführer A–Z.* Vol. II, No. 1. Ed. Kurt Böttcher et al. Berlin: Volk und Wissen, 1974. 132–135.

Lyotard, Jean-François. *The Differend. Phrases in Dispute.* Trans. Georges Van Den Abbeele. Minneapolis: U of Minnesota P, 1988.

Maaz, Hans-Joachim. "Zur psychischen Verarbeitung des Holocaust in der DDR." *Erinnerung. Zur Gegenwart des Holocaust in Deutschland-West und Deutschland-Ost.* Ed. Bernhard Moltmann et al. Frankfurt: Haag + Herchen, 1993. 163–168.

Markovits, Andrei S. and Beth Simone Noveck. "West Germany." *The World Reacts to the Holocaust.* Ed. David S. Wyman. Baltimore: The Johns Hopkins UP, 1996. 391–446.

Maser, Peter. *Glauben im Sozialismus.* Berlin: Gebr. Holzapfel, 1989.

Matusche, Alfred. *Der Regenwettermann.* In *Sozialistische Dramatik.* No ed. Berlin: Henschelverlag, 1968. 5–36.

Merrit, Richard L. "Politics of Judaism in the GDR." *Studies in GDR Culture and Society 9.* Ed. Margy Gerber, et al. Lanham: UP of America, 1989. 163–187.

Mertens, Lothar. "Der politische Umbruch in der DDR. Bemerkenswerte Stellungnahmen der jüdischen Gemeinden." *Tribüne* 113 (1990): 124–125.

———. "Schwindende Minorität. Das Judentum in der DDR." *Juden in der DDR*. Ed. Theodor Arndt et al. Duisburg: A. J. Brill, 1988. 125–159.

———. "Staatlich propagierter Antizionismus: Das Israelbild der DDR." *Jahrbuch für Antisemitismusforschung 2*. Ed. Wolfgang Benz. Frankfurt: Campus, 1993. 139–153.

Meuschel, Sigrid. *Legitimation und Parteiherrschaft in der DDR. Zum Paradox von Stabilität und Revolution in der DDR. 1945–1989*. Frankfurt: Suhrkamp, 1992.

Meyers Neues Lexikon. 2nd ed. Vol. I. Leipzig: Bibliographisches Institut, 1972.

Ministerium für Wissenschaft, Forschung und Kultur des Landes Brandenburg, ed. *Brandenburgische Gedenkstätten für die Verfolgten des NS-Regimes. Perspektiven, Kontroversen und internationale Vergleiche*. Berlin: Edition Hentrich, 1992.

Moltmann, Bernhard et al, eds. *Erinnerung. Zur Gegenwart des Holocaust in Deutschland-West und Deutschland-Ost*. Frankfurt: Haag + Herchen, 1993.

Monteath, Peter. "The Politics of Memory: Germany and its Concentration Camp Memorials." Paper delivered at the German Studies Association Conference, Chicago, September 1995.

Morsch, Günter, ed. *Von der Erinnerung zum Monument. Die Entstehungsgeschichte der Nationalen Mahn- und Gedenkstätte Sachsenhausen*. Berlin: Hentrich, 1996.

Muhlen, Norbert. *The Survivors. A Report on the Jews in Germany Today*. NY: Thomas Y. Crowell, 1962.

Müller, Heidi. *Die Judendarstellung in der deutschsprachigen Erzählprosa (1945–1981)*. 2nd ed. Königstein/Ts.: Hain, 1986.

Müller, Heiner. *Leben Gundlings Friedrich von Preußen Lessings Schlaf Traum Schrei*. Berlin: Henschelverlag, 1981.

Nachama, Andreas and Julius H. Schoeps, eds. *Aufbau nach dem Untergang. Deutsch-Jüdische Geschichte nach 1945. In memoriam Heinz Galinskis*. Berlin: Argon, 1992.

Neueste Zeit. Lehrbuch für den Geschichtsunterricht der Oberschule. Teil II. Berlin: Volk und Wissen, 1958.

Nieden, Susanne zur. "Das Museum des Widerstandskampfes und der Leiden des jüdischen Volkes." *Von der Erinnerung zum Monument. Die Entstehungsgeschichte der Nationalen Mahn- und Gedenkstätte Sachsenhausen.* Ed. Günter Morsch et al. Berlin: Hentrich, 1996. 272–278.

Niethammer, Lutz et al, eds. *Der "gesäuberte" Antifaschismus. Die SED und die roten Kapos von Buchenwald. Dokumente.* Berlin: Akademie, 1994.

Noll, Hans. "Früchte des Schweigens. Jüdische Selbstverleugnung und Antisemitismus in der DDR." *Deutschland Archiv* 22.7 (1989): 769–778.

O'Doherty, Paul. "German-Jewish Writers and Themes in GDR Fiction." *German Life and Letters* 49.2 (1996): 271–281.

———. *The Portrayal of Jews in GDR Prose Fiction.* Amsterdam: Rodopi, 1997.

Ostow, Robin. "Imperialist Agents, Antifascist Monuments, Eastern Refugees, Property Claims: Jews as Incorporations of East German Social Trauma, 1945–94." *Jews, Germans, Memory. Reconstructions of Jewish Life in Germany.* Ed. Michael Y. Bodemann. Ann Arbor: U of Michigan P, 1996. 227–241.

———. *Jews in Contemporary East Germany. The Children of Moses in the Land of Marx.* New York: St. Martin's, 1989.

———. "'The Persecution of the Jews by the Fascists': GDR Textbook Examples of Terror and Resistance in Presocialist Europe." Unpublished Manuscript.

Pätzold, Kurt. *Faschismus – Rassenwahn – Judenverfolgung. Eine Studie zur politischen Strategie und Taktik des faschistischen deutschen Imperialismus (1933–1935).* Berlin: Deutscher Verlag der Wissenschaften, 1975.

———, and Irene Runge. *Kristallnacht. Zum Pogrom 1938.* Cologne: Pahl-Rugenstein, 1988.

———. *Verfolgung, Vertreibung, Vernichtung. Dokumente des faschistischen Antisemitismus 1933–1942.* Frankfurt: Röderberg, 1984.

Paulus, Günter. *Die zwölf Jahre des Tausendjährigen Reiches. Streiflichter auf die Zeit der faschistischen Diktatur über Deutschland.* Berlin: Deutscher Militärverlag, 1965.

Peck, Jeffrey. "East Germany." *The World Reacts to the Holocaust.* Ed. David S. Wyman. Baltimore: The Johns Hopkins UP, 1996. 447–472.

Petzold, Joachim. *Faschismus. Regime des Verbrechens.* Berlin: Staatsverlag der DDR, 1984.

Probst, Lothar. "Deutsche Vergangenheiten — Deutschlands Zukunft. Eine Diagnose intellektueller Kontroversen nach der Wiedervereinigung." *Deutschland Archiv* 27.2 (1994): 173–180.

Rabinbach, Anton and Jack Zipes, eds. *Germans and Jews since the Holocaust.* New York: Holmes and Meier, 1986.

Rapoport, I. L. *The Doctors' Plot of 1953.* Cambridge, MA: Harvard UP, 1991.

Remarque, Erich Maria. *Der Funke Leben.* Cologne: Kiepenheuer und Witsch, 1988.

Richtlinien für den Unterricht in Deutscher Geschichte. Dritter Teil: Deutsche Geschichte in der neuesten Zeit. Ausgearbeitet von einer Gruppe demokratischer Lehrer im Auftrage der deutschen Zentralverwaltung für Volksbildung in der sowjetischen Besatzungszone. Berlin: Volk und Wissen, n.d. [1946].

Ritscher, Bodo. *Buchenwald. Rundgang durch die Gedenkstätte.* Erfurt: Druck Repro, 1986.

Röll, Wolfgang, ed. *Zur Neuorientierung der Gedenkstätte Buchenwald. Die Empfehlungen der vom Minister für Wissenschaft und Kunst des Landes Thüringen berufenen Historikerkommission.* Weimar: Weimardruck, 1992.

Rosenhaft, Eve. "The Uses of Remembrance." *Germans against Nazis: Essays in Honour of Peter Hoffmann.* Ed. Francis R. Nicosia and Lawrence D. Stokes. NY: Berg, 1990. 369–388.

Ross, Jonathan. "Remembering the Revolt: Stephan Hermlin's 'Die Zeit der Gemeinsamkeit' (1949)" *German Life and Letters* 49.2 (1996): 256–270.

Rother, Hans-Jörg. "Auftrag: Propaganda. 1960 bis 1970." *Schwarzweiß und Farbe. DEFA-Dokumentarfilme 1946–92.* Ed. Günter Jordan und Ralf Schenk. Potsdam: Jovis, 1996. 92–127.

Rothmann, Ottomar. "Die Nationale Mahn- und Gedenkstätte Buchenwald — Anmerkungen zur pädagogischen Arbeit." *Zur Arbeit in Gedenkstätten für die Opfer des Nationalsozialismus — ein internationaler Überblick.* Ed. Wulff E. Brebeck et al. Berlin: Aktion Sühnezeichen, 1988. 127–136.

Sartre, Jean-Paul. *Anti-Semite and Jew.* Trans. George J. Becker. New York: Schocken, 1975.

Schenk, Ralf. *Das zweite Leben der Filmstadt Babelsberg. DEFA-Spielfilme 1946–1992.* Potsdam: Henschel, 1994.

Schieber, Elke. "Anfang vom Ende oder Kontinuität des Argwohns. 1980 bis 1989." *Das zweite Leben der Filmstadt Babelsberg. DEFA-Spielfilme 1946–1992.* Ed. Ralf Schenk. Potsdam: Henschel, 1994. 264–327.

Schiller, Friedrich. *Kabale und Liebe.* F. Schiller. *Sämtliche Werke.* Vol. I. Ed. Gerhard Fricke and Herbert G. Göpfert. Munich: Hanser, 1958. 755–858.

Schlenstedt, Silvia. *Hermlin. Sein Leben und Werk.* Berlin: das europäische buch, 1985.

Schmelzkopf, Christiane. *Zur Gestaltung jüdischer Figuren in der deutschsprachigen Literatur nach 1945.* Hildesheim: George Olms, 1983.

Schmidt, Walter. "Jüdisches Erbe deutscher Geschichte im Erbe- und Traditionsverständnis der DDR." *Zeitschrift für Geschichtswissenschaft* 37.8 (1989): 692–714.

Schneider, Rolf. *Geschichte von Moischele.* R. Schneider. *Stücke.* Berlin: Henschelverlag, 1970. 209–278.

——. *Prozeß in Nürnberg.* Frankfurt: S. Fischer, 1968.

Schoeps, Julius H. and Dietmar Sturzbacher, eds. *Einstellung Jugendlicher in Brandenburg zu Juden und zum Staat Israel.* Potsdam: Brandenburgische Landeszentrale für politische Bildung.

Schüler, Thomas. "Das Wiedergutmachungsgesetz vom 14. September 1945 in Thüringen." *Jahrbuch für Antisemitismusforschung 2.* Ed. Wolfgang Benz. Frankfurt: Campus, 1993. 119–138.

Schultz, Hans Jürgen. *Mein Judentum.* Berlin: Kreuz, 1979.

Scrase, David. *Understanding Johannes Bobrowski.* Columbia: U of South Carolina P, 1995.

Seghers, Anna. *Das siebte Kreuz.* Berlin: Aufbau, 1946.

Semprun, Jorge. *Was für ein schöner Sonntag!* Frankfurt: Suhrkamp, 1984.

Seydel, Heinz, ed. *Welch Wort in die Kälte gerufen. Die Judenverfolgung des Dritten Reiches im deutschen Gedicht.* Berlin: Verlag der Nation, 1968.

Stein, Harry. *Juden in Buchenwald. 1937–1942.* Weimar: Weimardruck, 1992.

Steininger, Rolf. *Der Umgang mit dem Holocaust. Europa – USA – Israel.* Vienna: Böhlau, 1994.

Stern, Frank. "The Return to the Disowned Home — German Jews and the Other Germany." *New German Critique* 67 (1996): 57–72.

Stern, Susan, ed. *Speaking Out. Jewish Voices from United Germany.* Chicago: edition q, 1995.

Tabori, George. *Nathans Tod*. Munich: Bayrisches Staatsschauspielheft Nr. 79, 1990/91.

Thomalla, Ariane. "Von Ost-Berlin nach Straßburg. Gespräch mit der deutsch-jüdischen Schriftstellerin Barbara Honigmann." *Deutschland Archiv* 19.11 (1986): 1204–08.

Thompson, Jerry E. "Jews, Zionism, and Israel: The Story of the Jews in the German Democratic Republic since 1945." (Ph.D., Washington State University, 1978).

Timm, Angelika. "Israel in den Medien der DDR." *Jahrbuch für Antisemitismusforschung 2*. Ed. Wolfgang Benz. Frankfurt: Campus, 1993. 155–173.

——. "Der 9. November 1938 in der politischen Kultur der DDR." *Der Umgang mit dem Holocaust. Europa – USA – Israel*. Ed. Rolf Steininger. Vienna: Böhlau, 1994. 246–262.

Titze, Karl. "Einleitung." *Einstellung Jugendlicher in Brandenburg zu Juden und zum Staat Israel*. Ed. Julius H. Schoeps and Dietmar Sturzbacher. Potsdam: Brandenburgische Landeszentrale für politische Bildung, 1996. 10–11.

Turner, Henry. *German Big Business and the Rise of Hitler*. NY: Oxford UP, 1985.

Uhe, Ernst. *Der Nationalsozialismus in den deutschen Schulbüchern. Eine vergleichende Inhaltsanalyse von Schulgeschichtsbüchern aus der Bundesrepublik und der Deutschen Demokratischen Republik*. Bern: Lang, 1972.

Wander, Fred. "Brief an Primo Levi." *Sammlung 5: Jahrbuch für antifaschistische Literatur und Kunst*. Ed. Uwe Naumann. Frankfurt: Röderberg, 1982. 21–27.

——. *The Seventh Well*. Trans. Marc Linder. Berlin: Seven Seas, 1976.

——. *Der siebente Brunnen*. Berlin: Aufbau, 1971.

Wagner, Christa. *Geboren am See der Tränen*. Berlin: Militärverlag der Deutschen Demokratischen Republik, 1987.

Werle, Gerhard. "Der Holocaust als Gegenstand der bundesdeutschen Strafjustiz." *Erinnerung. Zur Gegenwart des Holocaust in Deutschland-West und Deutschland-Ost*. Ed. Bernhard Moltmann et al. Frankfurt: Haag + Herchen, 1993. 99–117.

Weiss, Peter. *Die Ermittlung*. Frankfurt: Suhrkamp, 1965.

Wolf, Christa. *Kindheitsmuster*. Berlin: Aufbau, 1976.

Wolf, Dieter. "Gesellschaft mit beschränkter Haftung." *Babelsberg. Ein Filmstudio 1912–1992*. No ed. Berlin: Argon, 1992. 247–270.

Wolf, Friedrich. *Professor Mamlock*. Leipzig: Reclam, 1980.

Wroblewsky, Vincent von. *Zwischen Thora und Trabant. Juden in der DDR*. Aufbau: Berlin, 1993.

Wyman, David S. *The World Reacts to the Holocaust*. Baltimore: The Johns Hopkins UP, 1996.

Young, James, ed. *The Art of Memory. Holocaust Memorials in History*. New York: Prestel, 1994.

——. *The Texture of Memory: Holocaust Memorials and Meaning in Europe, Israel, and America*. New Haven: Yale UP, 1993.

Zinner, Hedda. "Legitimer und legitimatorischer Antifaschismus. Zur Aufführungsgeschichte der *Ravensbrücker Ballade*." *Ravensbrücker Ballade oder Faschismusbewältigung in der DDR*. Ed. Klaus Jarmartz. Berlin: Aufbau, 1992. 175–204.

——. *Ravensbrücker Ballade*. H. Zinner. *Der Teufelskreis und andere Stücke*. Berlin: Der Morgen, 1986. 524–651.

"Zum Tode J.W. Stalins." *Sinn und Form* 5.2 (1953): 10–17.

Zweig, Arnold. *Die Feuerpause*. Berlin: Aufbau, 1954.

——. *Traum ist teuer*. Berlin: Aufbau, 1962.

Chronology of Films Cited

Feature Films

Die Mörder sind unter uns. Dir. Wolfgang Staudte. Soviet Occupation Zone, 1946.

Ehe im Schatten. Dir. Kurt Maetzig. Soviet Occupation Zone, 1947.

Affaire Blum. Dir. Erich Engel. Soviet Occupation Zone, 1948.

Zwischenfall in Benderath. Dir. Janos Veiczi. East Germany, 1956.

Der Prozeß wird vertagt. Dir. Herbert Ballmann. East Germany, 1958.

Sterne. Dir. Konrad Wolf. East Germany/Bulgaria, 1959.

Professor Mamlock. Dir. Konrad Wolf. East Germany, 1961.

Nackt unter Wölfen. Dir. Frank Beyer. East Germany, 1963.

Jetzt und in der Stunde meines Todes. Dir. Konrad Petzold. East Germany, 1963.

Chronik eines Mordes. Dir. Joachim Hasler. East Germany, 1965.

Ich war neunzehn. Dir. Konrad Wolf. East Germany, 1968.

Mord am Montag. Dir. Hans Kratzert. East Germany, 1968.

Der Mord, der nie verjährt. Dir. Wolfgang Luderer. East Germany, 1968.

Schüsse in Marienbad. Dir. Ivo Toman, Vaclav Gajer, Claus Dobberke. East Germany/Czechoslovakia, 1974.

Jakob der Lügner. Dir. Frank Beyer. East Germany, 1974.

Holocaust. Dir. M. J. Chomsky. USA, 1978.

Levins Mühle. Dir. Horst Seemann. East Germany, 1980.

Der Aufenthalt. Dir. Frank Beyer. East Germany, 1983.

Shoah. Dir. Claude Lanzmann. France, 1985.

Die Schauspielerin. Dir. Siegfried Kühn. East Germany, 1988.

Das schreckliche Mädchen. Dir. Michael Verhoeven. West Germany, 1990.

Documentary Films

Ein Tagebuch für Anne Frank. Dir. Joachim Hellwig. East Germany, 1959.

Mord in Łwow. Dir. Walter Heynowski. East Germany, 1960.

Aktion J. Dir. Walter Heynowski. East Germany, 1961.

Memento. Dir. Karlheinz Mund. East Germany, 1965.

Dawids Tagebuch. Dir. Konrad Weiß. East Germany, 1980.

Sonst wären wir verloren. Dir. Peter Rocha. East Germany, 1982.

Moses Mendelssohn. Ein Weltweiser aus Berlin. Dir. Maja Ulbrich/Donat Schober. East Germany, 1985.

Das Jahr 1945. Dir. Karl Gass/Klaus Wischnewski. East Germany, 1985.

Jeder konnte es sehen. Dir. Karl Gass/Klaus Wischnewski. East Germany, 1986.

Erinnern heißt leben. Dir. Roza Berger-Fiedler. East Germany, 1987.

Die Lüge und der Tod. Dir. Walter Heynowski/ Gerhard Scheumann/ Stephan Hermlin. East Germany, 1988.

Das Singen im Dom zu Magdeburg. Dir. Peter Rocha. East Germany, 1988.

Der Mann an der Rampe. Dir. Walter Heynowski/ Gerhard Scheumann. East Germany, 1989.

Befreier und Befreite. Dir. Helke Sander. Germany 1992.

Verschleppt ans Ende der Welt. Dir. Freya Klier. Germany, 1993.

Index